CHRISTIAN WISDOM *for* TODAY

CHRISTIAN WISDOM for TODAY

THREE CLASSIC STAGES OF SPIRITUALITY

Roger L. Ray

Chalice Press
St. Louis, Missouri

Cover design: Michael H. Domínguez
Cover photograph: Lynne Condellone
Interior design: Elizabeth Wright

This book is printed on acid-free, recycled paper.

Visit Chalice Press on the World Wide Web at
www.chalicepress.com

10 9 8 7 6 5 4 3 2 1   99 00 01 02 03 04

Library of Congress Cataloging–in–Publication Data

Ray, Roger L.
    Christian wisdom for today : three classic stages of spirituality / by Roger L. Ray
        p.   cm.
    Includes bibliographical references.
    ISBN 0-8272-0476-0
    1. Mysticism.   I. Title.
BV5082.2.R35 1998
248.2 — dc21   98-43550
                                                             CIP

Printed in the United States of America

Contents

Acknowledgments

Excerpts from THE SEVEN STOREY MOUNTAIN by Thomas Merton, copyright 1948 by Harcourt, Inc. and renewed 1976 by the Trustees of The Merton Legacy Trust, reprinted by permission of the publisher.

Excerpts from THE SPIRITUAL EXCERCISES OF ST. IGNATIUS by Anthony Mottola. Copyright © 1964 by Doubleday, a division of Bantam, Doubleday, Dell Publishing Group, Inc. Used by permission of Doubleday, a division of Random House, Inc.

Excerpts from THE IMITATION OF CHRIST by Thomas Kempis. Copyright © 1955 by Doubleday, a division of Random House, Inc. Used by permission of Doubleday, a division of Random House, Inc.

Excerpts from THE RULE OF ST. BENEDICT by Anthony C. Meisel. Copyright © 1975 by Anthony C. Meisel & M.L. Del Mastro. Used by permission of Doubleday, a division of Random House, Inc.

Excerpts from THE CLOUD OF UNKNOWING AND THE BOOK OF PRIVY COUNS by William Johnston. Copyright © 1973 by William Johnston. Used by permission of Doubleday, a division of Random House, Inc.

Excerpt from SOUL FRIEND by Kenneth Leech. Copyright © 1977 by Kenneth Leech. Introduction by J. M. Nouwen copyright © 1980 by Harper & Row, Publishers, Inc. Used by permission of HarperCollins Publishers, Inc.

Preface

How great a vanity it also is to desire a long life
and to care little for a good life.
Thomas à Kempis[1]

This is a book that grows out of a yearning of the heart—a yearning first experienced as a nebulous dissatisfaction with the place to which my own faith journey had led me—and a realization that something very vital was missing. My intent is to explore the process of spiritual growth, drawing on the ancient wisdom of Christian tradition and leading into the mystical dimension of faith.

My early experience of dissatisfaction might have been a crisis. After leaving the world of secular employment to enter seminary and serve a student parish, I found myself in the immensely uncomfortable position of being a spiritual leader who had a very unrewarding spiritual life. It had been tremendously rewarding at one time, but somewhere in the process of graduate school and parish work, something had changed.

I say that this could have been a crisis, but the crossroads where I had arrived turned out to have opened onto a veritable superhighway. My feeling was a fearful one, as if I had lost something that could not be recovered. But fortunately there was a vast amount of literature at this crossroads to indicate that my experience was a very common one, and that the real richness of the spiritual life was still ahead of me.

There comes a point in the faith journey when rationalism (what I think that I believe) and institutional religion (what I have been told to believe) cease to be rewarding. It is at this point that Christian people begin to look to the great spiritual guides of our faith to lead us in the direction of an existential dimension (something felt) of faith that transcends the purely rational expression of religion. The purpose of this book is to examine the process and resources for the journey into a broader experience of faith that lies in the direction of mystery. Obviously, this is not for the sole purpose of providing information. My ardent hope is that those who have given up on their spiritual life will find in these pages a reason to believe that there is something out there worth crossing the desert of spiritual dryness to find.

Readers will find fairly extensive quotes from spiritual classics. I hope that the material quoted will give readers confidence to read these classics for themselves. All biblical quotations are from the *New Revised Standard Version* except where otherwise noted. While the text that I have written does reflect our modern sensitivity to gender, many of the resources quoted are from an age of masculine-dominated language. In order to be true to the quoted texts, I have not taken the liberty of altering them, but I pray that we may still hear their voices for the insights they have to offer to the modern church.

I wish to express my gratitude for the many monks who have welcomed me and befriended me during my many years of visits to their monastic houses. I am also deeply grateful for the guidance and encouragement of one of my professors from many years ago, Dr. Liston Mills. Many thanks are due to the members of National Avenue Christian Church in Springfield, Missouri, who gave me enough time off from my pastoral duties to commit this work finally to paper. Finally, by way of dedication, I offer my thanks to my daughter, Valerie, whose arrival in my life has taught me more about love than any other teacher ever could.

CHAPTER 1

The Nature of the Problem

*Every day people are straying from the church and
going back to God.*

Lenny Bruce

Have you ever noticed that no matter how bad traffic
may be in your community on Monday through Friday,
on Sunday morning you can drive down almost any street
in town, unhindered by the congestion you encounter
during the week? In the city where I live, where Christianity would be the professed religion of nearly 90 per-
cent of our population, Sunday mornings are very quiet.

There are churches on nearly every corner. Persons of
every age and color find their way into houses of worship
all over town, but many more are attending the "church
of the Sunday paper" in their own backyards. They are
not atheists, nor are they necessarily more morally cor-
rupt than those who have stuffed themselves into uncomfortable clothes and made their way into their pews. Many
of those who are staying off the streets on Sunday mornings used to be churchgoers, but they have lost any sense
of a reason to go. Many would go if they believed that
there was anywhere worth going to.

1

It should also be noted that among those sitting in the pews are many people who are barely there. If friends had invited them down to the lake for the weekend, they would have accepted the invitation. If relatives were visiting from out of town, they would have stayed home. There are those for whom—and this may be the more serious lot—if one more offensive thing is said from the pulpit, in Sunday school, or in a board meeting…they're gone!

Both inside and outside our churches we are witnessing a kind of spiritual wasting away. None of this is lost on me. I have felt faith melting away from me like Icarus' wings, and I have known the cynicism and doubt of a Christian headed for the nearest door.

In that feeling, there is both good news and bad. The good news is that to experience spiritual dryness is not necessarily a sign of spiritual death, but rather a sign that it is time to move on—to discover what theologian Paul Tillich called "the big God who is beyond the little gods."

The bad news—the reason for all of the subsequent pages of this book—is that *real spirituality involves a journey*, a journey that requires hard work, patience, and a great deal of humility. The greatest deterrent to spiritual growth is temptation not to some wild, self-indulgent sin, but to laziness. The desire for a quick fix or an easy solution has led hosts of seekers down various pathways of false spirituality.

One of the differences between our religious language and the religious language of scripture, a theme to which I will uncomfortably return from time to time, is that we tend to talk about salvation as a past event. You will hear a person say, "I got saved when I was eleven years old." Similarly, many of our traditions look at baptism or confirmation as a kind of graduation ceremony. In scripture, salvation is never a past event but is always a journey, something that remains in progress, a process of becoming saved. Luke says rather matter-of-factly in his account of the early days of the church, "And day by day the Lord added to their number those who were being saved" (Acts 2:47b)—not "were saved" but "were being saved."

Even the apostle Paul, who was rarely shy in his spiritual claims, writes emphatically that our salvation is found in the lifelong pursuit of a journey of faith.

> Not that I have already obtained this or have already reached the goal; but I press on to make it my own, because Christ Jesus has made me his own. Beloved, I do not consider that I have made it my own; but this one thing I do: forgetting what lies behind and straining forward to what lies ahead, I press on toward the goal for the prize of the heavenly call of God in Christ Jesus. (Phil. 3:12–14)

The Fatal Divorce of Mind and Heart

Forms of Christian spirituality typically appeal either to the head or to the heart. One great spiritual director said that the goal of the Christian journey is for the mind to descend into the heart, a true marriage of intellect and experience—because, you see, God is not in your head, no matter how important that reason is to mature faith. And God is not contained or defined by your personal experiences, no matter how profound such experiences may be. We want both the mind (reason) and the heart (experience) together, with each governing and informing the other.

Most of us who have our faith roots in what has variously been called the "mainstream" or "old line" churches of America have been tremendously influenced by an appeal to the head. Rationalism, as an approach to faith, is not necessarily synonymous with an intellectual or scholarly faith. With the advent of the industrial and scientific advances of the eighteenth and nineteenth centuries, religion was often drawn increasingly into a tight rationalism, stressing the importance of what you believe over what you experience.

Although most of these older denominations have an early history with some very emotional revivals, they have often fallen prey to what is called a process of codification. An ancient spiritual parable that comes down to us in many forms tells of a day when an angel of light and the devil were watching a person walking on a road. The human bent over and picked something up. The devil asked, "What has the human found?"

"A piece of truth," the angel responded. "Doesn't it bother you now that the human creatures will have this piece of truth?"

"No," the devil answered, "because they will very soon make a belief out of it." Codification is the process of turning a living faith into a set of rules, behaviors, beliefs, or laws.

Jesus tells Nicodemus, "The wind blows where it chooses, and you hear the sound of it, but you do not know where it comes from or where it goes. So it is with everyone who is born of the Spirit" (Jn. 3:8). We have a tendency, as the parable suggests, to take every insight we gain about the spiritual life and try to turn it into a kind of spiritual law or "code of faith." But the Spirit, Jesus says, is like the wind. If you put the wind in a box, it is no longer wind, is it? We can feel the wind. We can follow it. But we cannot control it with laws and regulations.

The founders of my religious tradition, the Christian Church (Disciples of Christ), were very fond of the biblical reference "Come let us reason together" (Acts 17:2 KJV). They sought to rein in what they saw as the excesses of the emotionalism of frontier revivalism, but in so doing they also attempted to put the Spirit of God into a very small box. Those of my tradition must note the anything-but-subtle use of language by our founders, changing the use of the word *sacrament* (a gift of the presence of God) into an *ordinance* (a regulation or law to be obeyed). They would speak of those who had been baptized into the faith as persons who had been "obedient to the gospel."

I have tethered this modern codification to the coming of the industrial age, but it has come and gone through the centuries of the church's life. One reason why we presently know very little in the church about second- and third-century Christian writers is because that process of reducing faith into regulations was so common in that era. As the Anglican Bishop Kenneth Kirk writes in criticism of much of the historical church's production of legalistic documents:

> The vision of God is fading; and as it fades the characteristic dangers of Judaism come back, only thinly disguised by a veneer of Christian phrases. The process initiated by the "Didache" will be taken up by the Church Orders, the Councils of successive centuries, the prescripts of the "servant of the servants of God," the Penitential Books, until it finds its completion in the "Corpus Juris Canonici"—a monument of industry indeed, but a monument alike in conception and execution almost wholly of this world. By progressive codification Christianity (in Edward Meyer's appropriate phrase) is becoming "mechanized," as though it were a modern army; the Church is all but completely assimilated to the model of secular society.[1]

As I have mentioned, rationalism is not necessarily very scholarly or intelligent. It can simply be expressed as an inflexible fundamentalism—one of the paths to a simple but certain spirituality, fled to by some and fled from by others, but most certainly a form of modern idolatry of belief, destined to end far short of the absolute goal of the spiritual life. We do not speak much of heresy in the church of modern times, but at least some of those early identifications of false spirituality can be of help to us in the task at hand. I am thinking of a form of Christian heresy called "fideism," which is, simply put, a religion that draws its confidence from believing the right things.

This same heresy can be found in self-aggrandizing conservative groups who believe that they alone possess the truth about God (and hence have come to hold the keys to the kingdom), as well as in affluent congregations full of very educated professionals with an astonishingly intellectual and broad-minded preacher. (Liberals often elevate cynicism and doubt to the level of a sacrament—a form of pseudo-wisdom.) Still, God is not in our heads. The infinite cannot be apprehended by finite human reason, and the glory of God cannot be diagramed, defined, or put in a box. Reason is a necessary aid to a part of the spiritual journey, but the goal of the spiritual life will not be found in anyone's book of dogma. As Henri Nouwen has observed:

> During the last decade, many have discovered the limits of the intellect. More and more people have realized that what they need is much more than interesting sermons and interesting prayers. They wonder how they might really experience God.[2]

Just as we can assert that God is not in our heads, we can equally emphasize that simple experience cannot be made the goal of our spiritual journey either. "Below-the-neck" spirituality too easily ends up expressing itself in pietism, which Urban Holmes has characterized rather pointedly in this manner:

> Pietism is a term which, while historically rooted to the late seventeenth century, describes a degeneration of spirituality that may be characterized more generally as suffering from sentimentality, biblicism, personalism, exclusionism, fideism, anti-intellectualism, etc. It flourishes in self-congratulatory small groups. It is impervious to criticism because it recognizes no canon of truth outside the subjective meaning of its membership.[3]

The Neglect of the Greater Part of Faith:
The Mystery of God

The spiritual journey, as I am attempting to describe it, does not belong exclusively to either the conservative or the liberal camp of Christian thinking. In the nineteenth and twentieth centuries we find a substantive birth of biblical criticism and, as well, a proliferation of conservative theological writing. However, while those subscribing to higher biblical criticism and those who have embraced a biblical fundamentalism are opposed to each other, neither seemed to break out of the rationalism that would have allowed for a greater appreciation for that penetration of the mind into the heart. This union of mind and heart is something I want to express as *mysticism*.

It is quite possible that you have never heard the word *mystery* used in a positive context in church. I know that I didn't in my early life in the church. *Mystery* would have mostly been relegated to those who sought out Eastern or New Age religions. The above-the-neck spirituality of rationalists wants to understand, and mystery would seem to be in conflict with understanding.

Once again I defer to the apostle Paul who, in spite of some fairly strong tendencies toward pietism himself, uses the word *mystery* to describe our faith nearly twenty times in his biblical letters. That will become much clearer in later chapters. For now, let me simply say that the spiritual journey moves in a direction of a felt experience of faith that is *guided* by study and reason but moves into an acceptance of the transcendence of God that *cannot be known or understood*.

This is by no means a denial of reason. It is rather a faith that first climbs up and then stands on reason's shoulders. Like the old saying about the iceberg, what we can know of God is much less than the whole of God, and so we embrace and are embraced by a great mystery that is at the core of our experience of faith. Reason can help to guide our journey, but we will never find God in our own wisdom.

We could say that the common mistake of our modern time is that we are trying to substitute knowledge *about* God for knowledge *of* God. We cannot successfully divorce the science of theology from the experience of God and maintain a valid theology.

No matter how emphatically we must avoid the temptation toward fideism, we must never dismiss the absolute importance of sound theology. As my favorite philosopher, Søren Kierkegaard, said, "If you want to sew you must first tie a knot in your thread." That is to say, we cannot be entirely relativistic in our attempts to be open-minded and ecumenical. Theology has a vital place in the church and in our individual faith journey. In insisting that our experience of God must transcend our knowledge about God, I do not wish to minimize the damage done to our faith by the neglect of serious theology. I am very much in agreement with the theologian Leander Keck, who has recently written that "churches are suffering from theological anorexia."[4] As one modern proverb goes, "Modern theology is like a swimming pool where all the noise and splashing is coming from the shallow end."

Any gulf that exists between the practice of spirituality and the study of academic theology is certain to be deadly both to the spiritual seeker and to the theologian. The importance of personal study will be discussed at some length in later chapters, but let me also add here the observation that pastors need to be encouraged in their ministry as teachers, and that church members must be committed to serious study of what is being taught.[5] What could be more arrogant than to assume that we just "know" without study the things of God?

Pastoral Counseling as a Legitimizing Expression of Love

Perhaps prompted by a fear of being perceived as irrelevant by a world that has lost its interest in serious theology, we have seen a resurgence of interest in social action and a tremendous interest in pastoral counseling. Both are "causes" that bring new energy and purpose to the calling of the clergy. As valuable as both of these concerns are, they can also become rational replacements for existential spiritual life. This is a problem that Kenneth Leech describes so well in his book about spiritual direction, *Soul Friend*:

> Alas there is a great silence. Darkness has fallen upon us. The saints look at us through the mist of the past. We cannot understand their ways. The devils shrug their shoulders and have no comment. Only the sociologists and anthropologists talk endlessly in a new vocabulary…The psychologists too flatter our sense of self-importance, and we turn the church of God into a consulting room and trained counselors (Ulrich Simon).
>
> Amid the clinical trends in contemporary pastoral guidance, [the priest] will keep alive the permanent issues of sin and forgiveness. To be healthy and to be whole is no substitute for being penitent, forgiving, and holy (Michael Ramsey).[6]
>
> His statement is certainly true. The spread of interest in "pastoral counseling" and "pastoral clinical training," however desirable in itself, has certainly tended to lead to the neglect of confession and direction.

By the beginning of this century the whole of religion had come under cynical attack, but we had no biblical critic who became as plausible as religion's criticism from the world of psychology. Sigmund Freud and the growing science of psychology found a receptive audience for the dismissal of the relevance of faith. Their cause was furthered by the the fact that many of the accusations against the church were absolutely true! Rather than trying to rediscover the validity of our faith in the core of Christian witness and experience, we often began pandering for some new validating word from the field of psychology. As ministers began to create and preach a "gospel according to Freud," psychologists began lamenting the loss of the voice of genuine spirituality:

> In the 1930s Jung claimed that "about a third of my cases are suffering from no clinically definable neurosis, but from the senselessness and emptiness of their lives. It seems to me that this can well be described as the general neurosis of our time." To Laing…the loss of transcendence in our culture is indicative of its death. What we term "sanity" is in fact spiritual deprivation. True sanity involves the dissolution and the transcendence of the normal ego.[7]

When archaeologists discover the remains of what may have been a human settlement, one of the primary things that they look for in deciding if the find was of human origin is whether there is any evidence of religion. The human being is a spiritual creature. It is simply in us to seek some expression of transcendence. What a deep irony when we find psychologists (from whom we cringed in fear of condemnation) who sound like preachers as they bemoan the loss of a spiritual center in our time.

The Moral High Ground of Social Justice Advocacy

But just as clinical theology without experience becomes hollow, so do our attempts at social justice. Religion has always held the voice of moral imperative, and so, in a search for validity, it is natural that we would beat the drum for justice. But without the experience of faith there is no impetus behind our interest in ethics.

In his pre-monastery days, the great spiritual leader Thomas Merton gave up on the attempt to energize the meaning of his life purely through the philanthropic approach to social movements. He had sought to use communism as a replacement for the void of religion in his life. Bouncing from one social issue to another, but finally realizing that he could not be fully invested in any such concern, he accepted that he lacked any real purity of motive:

> And that was the end of my days as a great revo-
> lutionary. I decided that it would be wiser if I just
> remained a "fellow-traveler." The truth is that my
> inspiration to do something for the good of man-
> kind had been pretty feeble and abstract from the
> start. I was still interested in doing good for only
> one person in the world—myself.[8]

By attempting to own a genuine social conscience in the absence of an existential faith, it was as if we had "sold our birthright" as Christians.

Any honest reading of the Christian gospels will quickly reveal that a major portion of the preaching of Jesus had to do with social justice, the compassionate treatment of the poor and oppressed. The disappointing discovery that comes to virtually anyone who has worked with religious benevolent agencies is the shallowness of commitment such causes generally receive. We try to reinvigorate our Christian spirituality with social justice causes that should be immediately accepted as causes worthy of great personal commitment and sacrifice on the part of serious Christians, but most of what we can see in their financial reports is symbolic support from churches and individual Christians. Note how much government and foundation support is received even by such popular causes as Habitat for Humanity. Among those who work in relief agencies, we discover an ever-increasing percent-age of work done by paid staff members, VISTA workers, and students who are working for educational credits.

Pleas for the hungry and homeless rarely produce sus-tained commitment in the absence of a deeply experienced faith. Social activism alone will not keep faith alive. Social activism is properly the fruit of sincere faith, and sincere faith will produce fruit! James is frighteningly clear:

For judgment will be without mercy to anyone who has shown no mercy; mercy triumphs over judgment. What good is it, my brothers and sisters, if you say you have faith but do not have works? Can faith save you? If a brother or sister is naked and lacks daily food, and one of you says to them, "Go in peace; keep warm and eat your fill," and yet you do not supply their bodily needs, what is the good of that? So faith by itself, if it has no works, is dead. (Jas. 2:13–17)

A sincere and committed life in advocacy for the poor and oppressed is the appropriate response to faith. What I am pointing out is that social justice ministries have not succeeded in producing faith. First we must grow the tree before we can plan a harvest of fruit. Our commitment to justice ministries will never be deeper than our experience of faith for any sustained amount of time.

The Forest Obscures the Trees

This frustrated search for meaning in life is equally applicable to the clergy and laity, but it has a particular edge in the life of the minister. We were attracted to ministry specifically because our faith invigorated our lives with substance and meaning, but the very nature of the day-to-day tasks of ministry can become the enemy of realizing true spiritual relevance.

Just look for a moment at our daily routine. In general we are very busy people. We have many meetings to attend, many visits to make, many services to lead. Our calendars are filled with appointments, our days and weeks filled with engagements, and our years filled with plans and projects. There is seldom a period in which we do not know what to do, and we move through life in such a distracted way that we do not even take the time and rest to wonder if any of the things we think, say, or do are worth thinking, saying, or doing. We simply go along with the many "musts" and "oughts" that have been handed to us, and we live with them as if they were authentic translations of the gospel of our Lord. People must be motivated to come to church, youth must be entertained, money must be raised, and above all everyone must be happy.

These very compulsions are at the basis of the two main enemies of the spiritual life: anger and greed. Anger in particular seems close to a professional vice in the contemporary ministry. Pastors are angry at their leaders for not leading and at their followers for not following. They are angry at those who do not come to church for not coming and angry at those who do come for coming without enthusiasm. They are angry at their families, who make them feel guilty, and angry at themselves for not being who they want to be. This is not an open, blatant, roaring anger, but an anger hidden behind the smooth word, the smiling face, and the polite handshake. It is a frozen anger, an anger that settles into a biting resentment and slowly paralyzes a generous heart.[9]

We will return to the other main enemy of the spiritual life, greed, at the beginning of chapter 4.

For those of you who have come to the conclusion that your pastor is not a spiritual person, there are two things you may need to consider. The first is that you may very well be right. The second is that the church itself may have been the chief murderer of her or his spiritual life. We must value prayer, meditation, and study to such a degree that we expect it of our spiritual leaders. For many years I have had an agreement with the church I serve that I will go away to a monastery for retreat every three months. This is my time to study, pray, and keep my own spiritual life on track. It is indicative of how these retreats are viewed that I am asked upon return, "Did you have a nice vacation?" Even within the church we have come to define staff meetings, board and committee meetings, letter-writing, addressing newsletters, and setting up tables and chairs as pastoral "work," but study, prayer, and meditation are viewed as "vacation."

The mundane must not be allowed to crowd out the crucial. The mechanics of operating a church must not be allowed to assassinate the reason for the church's existence. Spiritual leaders must take time, in a disciplined way, to nurture their own spiritual journey, or we will all suffer from their loss.

The Prodding of Pain and Emptiness

Up to this point I have been attempting to articulate the spiritual wasting away that so many of us have felt at one time or another. As painful as this spiritual depression is, such depression is not always bad. Depression often is caused by our resistance to change. It is the result of an inner conflict between the part of ourselves that is crying out to move on and the part of ourselves that is resistant and dug in. In fact, spiritual depression may simply be the "wake-up call," the motivation to move on to something more.

In recent years, James Fowler has made a great contribution to our understanding of the spiritual journey in his book *The Stages of Faith*. In it, Fowler sees this spiritual depression coming at the juncture of movement from an institutional religion into a new and very healthy appreciation for mysticism.

> Elements from a childish past, images and energies from a deeper self, a gnawing sense of the sterility and flatness of the meanings one serves—any or all of these may signal readiness for something new. Stories, symbols, myths and paradoxes from one's own or other traditions may insist on breaking in upon the neatness of the previous faith. Disillusionment with one's compromises and recognition that life is more complex than Stage

4's logic of clear distinctions and abstract concepts can comprehend, press one toward a more dialectical and multileveled approach to life truth.[10]

Sadly, the church has generally failed to offer any real assistance to those who become "stuck" in their spiritual journey. We have been like the lunch counter in the old *Saturday Night Live* shows where the whole menu consisted of cheeseburgers and Pepsi. Order anything else and you are greeted with confusion. In the church, we have fostered a "one note" spirituality that asks our members to live on cheeseburgers and Pepsi for the rest of their lives.

When faced with the onset of a dryness of faith, many people will drop out of church; others will find a different church. Some authors have talked a great deal about church nostalgia as a response to the death of their faith. Such persons demand that we "sing the good old hymns" and bemoan the passing of the great preachers of their youth because they remember a time when their faith was alive and had meaning, and they want that time to come back by repeating what they associate with those memories, without understanding that it is not so much the church that has changed but it is *they* who are ready to move forward. No amount of moving backward will ever effect the desired result of spiritual nostalgia. The only way is forward into something higher that will inevitably involve sacrifice of some of what we cherish in our memories.

Of course, there are also those who turn their spiritual hunger into a quest for something worse than the same old cheeseburgers and Pepsi. When the church has failed to own its heritage of transcendence, many have groped for shallow substitutes. Andre Godin has observed:

> The loss of an experience of the divine through cosmic reality and the mistrust of any religious experience described as "Erlebnis" (emotion felt) are culturally inevitable but are a cause for regret. Many people in our culture who have become or remained nonbelievers turn, with a fascination

which reveals their wish to believe in them, to reputedly marvelous phenomena: unidentified flying objects (UFOs), astrology, looking into the future through "clairvoyant" experiences, spiritualism, cures hastily designated as miraculous because they occur outside the framework of medicine.[11]

But, Godin continues, there is a new hope for the church of today that is again opening its arms to embrace a genuine experience of the living God:

There has perhaps been too much mistrust of religious experience these last thirty years. In our increasingly secularized society this has probably been the case for much longer—but what about in the churches? The tendency seems to be reversed at present. The word "experience" has regained prestige, along with its synonyms in everyday language: living intensely moments of vivid consciousness, the testimony of the witness of this experience in all its subjectivity.[12]

I believe that many modern Christians are very ready to take a new look at the traditional path of spiritual growth. The very nature of the journey makes it difficult to express in words, and yet that is exactly what we must try to do. As Urban Holmes says,

We speak of God, and in so doing identify, clarify, and share the experience of God. But language is historical. There is always a longing in persons of deep prayer to get behind the finite forms of language to the infinite God, who is ineffable—i.e., he cannot be described by language. This tension exists in any experience of prayer. The mystics will say to us that they cannot describe what they have experienced. Yet they try, and it is never enough.[13]

CHAPTER 2

Where Are We Going?

Blessed are the pure in heart, for they will see God.
Matthew 5:8

I have been quite emphatic in saying that the spiritual life is a journey, but we never set out on a journey unless we believe we're going somewhere. Where does the spiritual journey take us? What is our goal in pursuing a religious life?

Since so much of our goal in the spiritual life is beyond thought, knowledge, or mere words, it becomes a bit ironic to try to talk about it. One of my favorite professors used to state frankly that we were trying to "eff" the ineffable! I have referred to mystical theology and the transcendent experience of God, but trying to describe in some detail just what this is about is a very difficult thing to do. As it is in many such cases, it is easier to say what a thing "is not" than it is to say what it "is."

Every child is familiar with the cartoon images of heaven and hell: white-robed angels with giant wings who are walking on clouds and playing a harp, and dark caves full of fire and smoke with bat-winged demons carrying pitchforks. Just because we can conjure up such ridiculous images does not, of course, mean that the literal images of the ultimate rewards and punishments of the religious life are necessarily equally absurd, and yet such images are indicative of what may be the most dangerous misconception of the spiritual journey.

The Motivations of Fear and Lust, Now and Then

There is certainly no shortage of witnesses to the conviction that the goal of the religious life is the reward of eternal life in heaven, either in modern thought or in the writings of the ancient world. The second-century theologian Tertullian, who shaped so much of Latin theology, describes the motives for the Christian life as "fear and hope—eternal fire and eternal life."[1]

And even though the sixth-century *Rule of St. Benedict* has been the standard guide for the high calling of the monastic life, we find elements in it that are also none too idealistic. Among the works that Benedict describes as the instruments of a monk's good works (a list that begins with a synopsis of the Ten Commandments but continues to become a list of seventy-two instructions!) are:

44. To fear Judgment Day.
45. To fear Hell.
46. To desire eternal life with all one's spirit.[2]

And the great spiritual director and author of the sixteenth-century classic *The Spiritual Exercises*, Saint Ignatius of Loyola, takes a no less self-interested approach to the goal of the religious life, blatantly saying over and over again, "Man is created to praise, reverence, and serve God our Lord, and by this means to save his soul."[3]

Ignatius was a mystic and reformer of the Catholic Church in the early days of the Protestant Reformation.

While healing from a wound received in battle, Ignatius reported having a series of visions of the Virgin Mary, who led him in the writing of his book of spiritual exercises. This literal manual for a forty-day retreat was intended to help those who made the retreat to discover a sense of vocational calling to be a monk. In his introduction, Ignatius connects the following of the exercises with the goal of eternal reward:

> Spiritual exercises are methods of preparing and disposing the soul to free itself of all inordinate attachments, and after accomplishing this, of seeking and discovering the Divine Will regarding the disposition of one's life, thus insuring [*sic*] the salvation of his soul.[4]

This is very much in line with the mechanical approach to religion mentioned in the preceding chapter. In the process of codification we identify certain rules that, when followed correctly, produce the desired result, which in this case is eternal reward. Tertullian even goes so far as to say, "If we do well, we merit of God, and He becomes our debtor."[5]

In the sixteenth century, Thomas à Kempis, author of the spiritual classic *The Imitation of Christ*, writes as though Christ were speaking in the first person regarding self-denial and ultimate reward:

> In what, then, Lord, does true perfection stand? It stands in a man offering all his heart wholly to God, not seeking himself or his own will, either in great things or in small, in time or in eternity, but abiding always unchanged and always yielding to God equal thanks for things pleasing and displeasing, weighing them all in one same balance, as in His love. And if he is so strong in God that when inward consolation is withdrawn he stirs his heart to suffer more, if God so will, yet does not justify

himself or praise himself as holy and righteous, then he walks in the very true way of peace, and may well have a sure and perfect hope that he will see Me face to face in everlasting joy in the kingdom of heaven. And if he can come to a perfect and full contempt and despising of himself, then he will have a full abundance of rest and peace in joy everlasting, according to the measure of his gift.[6]

From Self-interest to Something More

To say that the spiritual life is a journey necessarily implies that there is a "starting place," and that before we arrive at the goal there may be many "in-between places." That is to say, the place where we begin to make our journey may not be a very good place to be, but you must begin wherever you are, and it is from that place that you set out in a new direction. The point where we all begin, from birth, is selfishness. An infant cries when she or he is wet, or hungry, or sleepy, or bored. An infant does not care about what else you may be doing or how tired, hungry, sleepy, or bored you may be. An infant desires personal satisfaction above all else.

Some people from the social sciences suggest that the human creature never really gets beyond being entirely motivated by the goal of personal satisfaction; rather we simply become more sophisticated in the ways in which we cry out for satisfaction. We learn the manners of social interaction so that we can effectively manipulate our environment and relationships to serve a self-satisfying end. This same level of motivation is brought to religious life. The place where most of us start in our faith journey is a very selfish one.

Our initial reason for being religious may be to avoid the punishment of hell and to gain the reward of heaven. We may begin, at an early age, to couch those desires in less self-interested language, but the basic form of the motivation remains.

The notion that religious life is some kind of "divine fire insurance" may be a beginning place, but it is a motivation that must eventually be dismissed in order to move beyond it to something higher. Kenneth Kirk sought to define the issue, borrowing from the language of Irenaeus, who defined the goal of religious life as follows: "The glory of God is a living man; and the life of man is the vision of God."[7] Rejecting selfishness as the plausible goal of spirituality, Kirk writes:

> The primary question of all formal ethics is the definition of the *summum bonum* [the greatest good]. Is it best defined in terms of "happiness" (reward) or in terms of "virtue" (duty)?
>
> For those who accept this fundamental axiom of Christian ethics, which on the one hand repudiates emphatically all forms of hedonism (even the most spiritual), but refuses to lend itself to the extremes of Quietism on the other, the words "disinterestedness" or "unselfishness" express the ideal of Christian character.
>
> The first practical question for Christian ethics is, therefore, How is disinterestedness, or unselfishness, to be attained? Once granted that moralism, or formalism, cannot bring the soul nearer to it, and there remains only one way—the way of worship. Worship lifts the soul out of its preoccupation with itself and its activities, and centers its aspirations entirely on God.[8]

Clearly, a mature spirituality transcends enlightened self-interest, which expresses itself in fear of hell and lust for heaven. However, even though the language of the fear of hell and lust for heaven is present in most of the ancient classical writings of spirituality, we find in them much evidence of an awareness that this is not the ultimate goal of the spiritual life. Perhaps their use of the language of divine reward and punishment is also related to the difficulty of expressing the higher sense of a more disinterested[9] union with God; perhaps they also were aware that their readers would virtually all be at a beginning place of self-interest in their journey, but that they would grow into something more.

In the World but Not of It

Much of the direction in spirituality begins with talk about piety and self-denial. That fact, taken with a lot of talk about an "inward" life, can be interpreted to mean that the ultimate goal of spirituality has something to do with denial of the world and everything in it. That perception is mistaken. The process of growth transcends physical experience but does not necessarily condemn the physical world. The communion with God that we seek is not found simply in "a repudiation of sensible reality through the inward journey within the self and then to the God who is beyond self."[10]

The tools of asceticism (spiritual exercises of self-denial) are used to focus the pilgrim on the attainment of the goal of spiritual union. As Anthony Meisel and M. L. del Mastro say in their introduction to their translation of *The Rule of St. Benedict*, "Monasticism is the quest for union with God through prayer, penance, and separation from the world, pursued by those who share a communal life."[11]

Mystical theology is not at all inherently devoted to a view that the spiritual world and the physical world are at war with one another.[12] We shall see in the final pages of this book that the exercises of self-abnegation (practices of self-denial leading to a kind of self-loathing or hatred of the flesh) are transformed in the life of the spiritually mature in the traditions of both the East and the West. However, the affirmation of the created world is considerably more evident in the writings from the Eastern traditions.

In the Western world, we have come to think of our salvation as having to do with our individual soul's finding redemption in heaven, which is often expressed as an almost "eternal suburban neighborhood." Eastern spiritual writers take a much broader view, seeing our salvation in terms of the redemption of the entire cosmos. The whole subject of our rugged individualism as it is expressed in our theology will be the subject of more detailed consideration later.

Love Is the Answer!

Beyond a faith motivated by either fear or self-interest and beyond a simple faith of satisfying the pietistic expectations of a controlling god, there is a way of reaching higher than our intellect can grasp. That way is the way of loving. This is nowhere better exemplified than in the writing of the anonymous author of the fourteenth-century classic of mystical theology, *The Cloud of Unknowing*:

> For the intellect of both men and angels is too small to comprehend God as he is in himself. Try to understand this point. Rational creatures such as men and angels possess two principal faculties, a knowing power and a loving power. No one can fully comprehend the uncreated God with his knowledge; but each one, in a different way, can grasp him fully through love. Truly this is the unending miracle of love: that one loving person, through his love, can embrace God, whose being fills and transcends the entire creation. And this marvelous work of love goes on forever, for he whom we love is eternal. Whoever has the grace to appreciate the truth of what I am saying, let him take my words to heart, for to experience this love is the joy of eternal life while to lose it is eternal torment.[13]

In the concluding thoughts of this classic piece of spiritual direction, the language of reward and punishment is still present but in a much more palatable fashion. The reward is couched in the language of the experience of love *for* or *of* or *in* God. If we talk about *union* with God, we cannot escape talk about *love*.

The great spiritual mystics speak of love as the ultimate test of genuine spirituality:

> Love is always the primary test of the mystical life. "In the evening they will examine thee in love," says St. John. St. Teresa adds, "it is not a matter of thinking a great deal but of loving a great deal— so do whatever arouses you most to love."[14]

Thomas à Kempis, in *The Imitation of Christ*, writes a veritable "ode to love":

> Love is a great and good thing, and alone makes heavy burdens light and bears in equal balance things pleasing and displeasing. Love bears a heavy burden and does not feel it, and love makes bitter things tasteful and sweet. The noble love of Jesus perfectly imprinted in man's soul makes a man do great things, and stirs him always to desire perfection and to grow more and more in grace and goodness.
>
> Love will always have a man's mind raised to God and not occupied with the things of the world. Love will also be free from all worldly affection, so that the inward sight of the soul is not darkened or hindered, and a man's affection toward heavenly things is not banished from his will by inordinate winning or losing of worldly things. Nothing, therefore, is sweeter than love; nothing higher, nothing stronger, nothing larger, nothing more joyful, nothing fuller, nothing better, in heaven or on earth, for love descends from God, and may not finally rest in anything lower than God. Such a lover flies high; he runs swiftly, he is merry in God, he is free in soul. He gives all for all, and has all in all, for he rests in one high Goodness above all things, from whom all goodness flows and proceeds. He beholds not only the gifts, but the Giver above all gifts.[15]

From Simply Loving to Uniting Lovers

Here we come to the most difficult, and therefore the most delicate, aspect of trying to describe the absolute goal of the spiritual journey. The first step needs fairly little defense, as it would seem clear to anyone who considers it—that love for God is a higher motivation than fear of punishment or greed for the riches of heaven. But if we are to move toward God in love, where does this journey find its completion?

The goal of the spiritual life is union with God. This unitive experience refers to a dimension of spirituality that need not be in conflict with either "liberal" or "conservative" theology. Mystical theology is neither dependent upon nor exclusive of the differing perspectives of faith. As seen earlier, the spiritual classics throughout the past centuries can reflect a quite literal view of the dogma of the church while giving instruction in the journey toward a mystical experience of God. Dogma is not irrelevant, as we will see in a later chapter, but the several paths of Christian thought can converge into an experience of God that transcends thought and is somehow seated in the emotion of love.

Mystical theology is not so much a denial of sensory pleasure as it is an affirmation of the experience of union with God that is ultimately attained in an inward journey. I must ask you to consider very carefully what I am about to say: God's "communion" with humans actually makes us part of God. We hear of this most clearly through the voices of Eastern Christianity, as Kenneth Leech summarizes the perspective of this body of thinkers in *Soul Friend*:

> In Eastern Christian thought, all theology is mystical. The description "theologian" is reserved for St. John, St. Gregory Nazianzen and St. Simeon, all of them exponents of the life of union and communion with God. The purpose of all theology is deification (theosis). There is, in the words of Irenaeus, a "participation (metoche) in God." "If

the Word is made man, it is that men might become gods." Origen too speaks of deification: the spirit is "deified by that which it contemplates." St. Athanasius also speaks of man's deifying through the vision of God, and this tradition is enriched in the Alexandrian school, particularly in St. Cyril of Alexandria (370-444). St. John of Damascus says that man was created for deification. St. Gregory of Nyssa says that "God has made us not simply spectators of the power of God, but also participants in his very nature." So, in Lossky's words, "No one who does not follow the path of union with God can be a theologian. The way of the knowledge of God is necessarily the way of deification." This is not some fringe sectarian belief; it is absolutely central to Orthodox theology and to all Orthodox spirituality.[16]

Interestingly, the popular twentieth-century Christian psychiatrist M. Scott Peck says much the same thing in his writing about the ultimate goal of spiritual growth in *The Road Less Traveled*:

> Why does God want us to grow? What are we growing toward? Where is the end point, the goal of evolution? What is it that God wants of us? It is not my intention here to become involved in theological niceties, and I hope the scholarly will forgive me if I cut through all the ifs, ands, and buts of proper speculative theology. For no matter how much we may like to pussyfoot around it, all of us who postulate a loving God and really think about it eventually come to a single terrifying idea: God wants us to become Himself (or Herself or Itself). We are growing toward godhood. God is the goal of evolution.[17]

We Are Not God Nor Are We "Gods"

This conversation about growing into a union with God demands some careful clarification. Just as I have previously mentioned, we come into the world as absolutely self-centered creatures, and that self-centeredness can assert and reassert itself in our lives and faith in increasingly sophisticated and deceptive ways. If we are not very careful, our language that expresses our love for God can evolve into subtle praise of ourselves.

Kenneth Kirk has said that the only vehicle toward a love of God that transcends self-interest is worship. But note how, in the past decades, even worship has come to focus less and less on God and more and more on the people gathered in worship. The only appropriate object of our worship is God, and therefore the only audience of worship is God. We are the worshipers and God is the worshiped. And yet much of what we hear in advocacy of reform in liturgy has to do with catering to the tastes of those who attend worship services. We demand to sing our favorite songs and often include songs in worship that actually address the people in the sanctuary rather than God. We ask for "helpful" sermons that might more appropriately appear in a newspaper advice column.

Count the personal pronouns in some of our favorite hymns. I grew up singing "In the Garden," which uses "I," "me," or "my" twelve times! A creeping personalism in our religious expressions has attempted to bring God down to us—or, more likely, to elevate our own importance to the level of a deity. No one speaks about this more earnestly than Leander Keck:

> In Paul's words, people "exchanged the glory of the immortal God for images resembling a mortal human being or birds or four footed animals or reptiles" (Romans 1:23). In other words, praise was directed toward the non-God as if it were God. Instead of inferring that the created is not the Creator, humanity reified the creator and deified the

creature, thereby exchanging truth for falsehood while claiming it was truth. As a result, everything else went wrong, and stays wrong until made right by God.[18]

This tendency toward deification of our own intentions can be seen most clearly in much of what is now called "New Age" religion, which focuses much of its mythology on illusions of personal empowerment. I do not want to dismiss the more legitimate aspects of the recovery of spiritual wisdom from Native American and certain Eastern traditions, because Christians should never be so arrogant as to assume that we have nothing to learn from the spiritual wisdom of other traditions. What is sad to me is that many of the better attempts at recovering and making such traditional wisdom available to a modern audience are often found in the same company in our bookstores as texts of far lesser import. Attempts at a spiritual life that are all self-promoting and free of challenge to personal transformation will not satisfy that legitimate spiritual hunger we recognize. Forgive me if I claim that much of what passes for modern expressions of spirituality is, in a word, embarrassing.

But dare we examine the personalism in the language of the mainstream churches? This is going to hurt. But what is this question that appears in one form or another in so many of our churches, a question asked of nearly every person coming to join our churches: "Do you accept Jesus Christ as your personal savior?" Take a moment and look through the New Testament for any example of a person accepting Jesus Christ as his or her personal savior. There is none!

In fact, look in your concordance for an occurrence of the word "personal" in the Bible. It is not there! In the whole two thousand pages of our scripture, not one writer thought that "personal" was an important enough concept so much as to utter the word! Why, then, has it become so important to us? As G. K. Chesterton observed when this tendency toward personalism was first growing strong, "A man can no more possess a private religion than he can possess a private sun and moon."[19]

All of that being said, I must add that there is obviously a personal dimension to our relationship with God, since God knows each of us individually as well as collectively. My point is that we do not change God to meet our personal desires, appetites, wishes, or opinions. God is God, and we are not God.

In the spiritual journey, we are moving toward God in love with God. Loving God changes us as we mature, so that our "personal" self becomes less rigid and we are more conformed to the mind and character of God.

All analogies break down if they are carried too far, but let me suggest that we think of our relationship with God as being something like the relationship of a rain drop to a rain cloud. God creates us with a bit of God's own spirit, as a cloud creates a raindrop that falls to earth. On the earth the drop of water has a life of its own apart from the cloud. It is changed. It may become a part of a tree, a river, an animal. But in time it is again released into the air, evaporated, and taken up into the cloud. In the cloud, it does not retain individuality but is united with the cloud and all other raindrops pulled up from the earth.

As I said, I do not want to carry this analogy too far, because I am not wanting to suggest a cycle of reincarnation, nor am I suggesting that we take a nihilistic view of our own existence. I do want to stress that the closer we come to union with God, the less important our personal distinctiveness becomes to us.

The goal of the spiritual journey is union with God. This is the greatest good and the purpose behind our creation. Recognizing the effective ineffability of the subject, we describe it variously as "existential," "mystical," "transcendent," "unitive," or, to repeat Kenneth Kirk's favored choice, "the vision of God."

When Do We Get There?

Whether this goal is completely attainable in this life or not is certainly debated. "On this point St. Thomas can speak without a moment's hesitation. The intuitive vision of the divine essence—the sight of God face to face—is sternly reserved for eternity."[20]

Thomas à Kempis also seems to suggest that the fullest experience of God requires a release of mortal life:

> My son, when you feel that a desire of everlasting bliss is given to you and that you desire to leave the tabernacle of your mortal body, so that you might clearly, without shadow, behold my clarity, then open your heart, and with all the desire of your soul receive that holy inspiration. And give greatest thanks to the high goodness of God that works so worthily for you, so graciously visits you, so fervently stirs you, and so mightily bears you up in order that you do not fall down to earthly pleasures by your own weight.[21]

The author of *The Cloud of Unknowing*, who divides the spiritual journey into four steps, also states clearly that the final part of the journey cannot be finished in this life, "but the fourth, though begun here, shall go on without ending into the joy of eternity."[22] And yet the experience is at least partially attainable in this life; to this fact the centuries of mystic witnesses attest.

That an attainment of the goal is possible is the hope held out to everyone who begins the journey. The question that lies before us is, "How does this journey proceed?"

CHAPTER 3

The Known Steps of the Journey

I remember clearly the night that I finished my seminary degree. It was a cold and drizzly December evening in Nashville, Tennessee, when a friend and I had driven to Vanderbilt to turn in my very last paper. After all of the frenzy of working to put myself through undergraduate school and divinity school, after listening to lectures for years, after reading and writing literally thousands of pages of papers, I stood on the eve of my ordination into the ministry and felt as empty and cold as the dark, damp air that shrouded the divinity school like the setting of a bad horror movie.

The simple faith that had led me to seminary in the first place was all gone, exposed for all of the myth, magic, superstition, and silly naivete that it generally was. But I knew that whatever I was supposed to have inside of me, which I was to share from the pulpit and altar of the church for the rest of my life, was nowhere to be found. My education had given me a lot of information, and I am deeply grateful to my professors for what I did learn in graduate school. What I was missing was a confidence and courage of faith that seemed to be so necessary to me both personally and professionally.

One thing I did hold onto. During the course of my education I had taken two weeks off to visit Israel. My initial interest was purely historical. But while I was there, one evening when I had gone into the old city alone, I stood outside the tomb of the Church of the Holy Sepulcher and listened to evening worship services being conducted in the several chapels arrayed around the tomb.

None of the services were in English. And yet, somehow, in the midst of that special place, in the dim smoky candlelight, listening to the chanting of prayers and hymns from several different directions, something happened to me—not a vision, not an ecstatic experience, but a felt certainty of the presence of God. It was, for me, a first taste of mystery, a gift from God, a drop that fell from heaven that somehow let me know that there was, somewhere, an ocean.

A Rediscovery of Ancient Wisdom

For most Christians, churched and unchurched, ordained and laity, what you are about to read will be new material. I do not say this with the triumphant tones of an Indiana Jones who has just discovered some great secret hidden for centuries in a long-lost tomb. Sadly, some of the greatest insights in guiding Christians in the spiritual life have been sitting in plain view, on the shelves of our libraries, undisturbed, unread, as if they were lost to us.

Two centuries of seekers have turned away from the institutional representations of the Christian faith and gone in search of a higher truth in Eastern religions, in science, in Native American spirituality, and in the theological voodoo of trendy psycho-spiritual movements, without ever realizing that we were in grave danger of losing a virtually limitless resource of Christian spirituality—lost to amnesia and neglect.

In honesty, I believe that it deserves to be said that some of our more famous modern athiests and agnostics were not so much rejecting the Christian faith as they were rejecting the Christian church. My own generation often became obsessed with innovative forms of spirituality because we did not believe that there was anything worthwhile in our own tradition. A careful reading of Mark Twain's work, for example, would betray a man of deep spiritual insight whose disparaging remarks about persons of faith should not be seen as anything less than the rather more scholarly attacks on the nature of the church broadly heralded in the work of such scholars as Søren Kierkegaard.

What needs to be said is simply that we have often abandoned the wealth of our tradition before we actually opened the last door to the treasury. An amazingly coherent yet profoundly rich tradition of spiritual wisdom lies before us, awaiting our rediscovery.

As diverse as the expressions of the Christian religion are, it is quite remarkable that there is a great deal of agreement on the process by which Christian people proceed in the spiritual journey. Writings on this subject from several periods of history modify, in one way or another, the description of the way to the goal of the spiritual life. But a basic structure continues to arise from the absolute majority of witnesses from the first century of the common era right up to the beginning of the Protestant Reformation.

The way follows a path of repentance, instruction, and love of or experience of God. These three primary stages have been called by many names, but the most common are *purgative*, *illuminative*, and *unitive*. Do not be alarmed if you have never heard these terms before. I was an ordained minister with nearly thirty years of faithful church attendance and I had never even heard the concepts discussed. However, a careful reading of the spiritual writers of the Christian faith reveals an awareness of the three steps (or ways) throughout the history of Christian thought. We find the concepts in the writings of Clement of Alexandria, Origen, Dionysius, Augustine, Bernard, and Bonaventure, to mention only a few of the more prominent ones.

Urban Holmes, in *A History of Christian Spirituality*, suggests that the three steps may be borrowed from a pre-Christian source:

> Maximus the Confessor (c. 580–662)...was the first to give the classical form to the three ways to God—purgation, illumination, and union—which became the classic "ladder" for Western medieval spirituality. Bonaventure (1221–1274) particularly will build on them. Actually the three steps under different names go back to Origen, and before him to Philo, who probably got it from the Greeks. The three ways are related to the prayer of the lips, mind, and the heart of the Eastern monks. Maximus was strongly influenced by Evagrius Ponticus even though he describes him as that "abominable heretic." He was, in effect, an instrument for Evagrius' unknown influence in later centuries.[1]

A more historically broad attestation to the three steps (or ways) could hardly be hoped for. It is important to note as well that even though these specific terms are not used in scripture, an awareness of the nature of spiritual development pervades the Bible.[2] Like the doctrine of the Trinity (which is also not specifically stated in scripture), the three traditional stages of the spiritual journey, once understood, become a way of seeing, a way of understanding where we are and where we are going.

In most instances, when we encounter references to more steps than these three, a close comparison of them reveals that different writers are making subdivisions of one of the three steps. *The Cloud of Unknowing* speaks of a journey of four steps, and the writings of John of the Cross and Teresa of Avila speak of ten or seven. It would seem that the great mystics had a great deal more to say about their experiences of union with God and would therefore include more "steps" within the unitive experience, but their teachings certainly do not contradict the assumed movement from confession to learning and practice toward a uniting with God. There is a logic to this movement that feels as natural to us as breathing in and breathing out. To begin the work of a spiritual birth, we must purge our lives of that which stands between ourselves and God (the purgative way). Then we must put into practice that which has been identified as the Christian life (learning through the illuminative way). And we will then have prepared the soil of our souls for God to plant within us the seeds of God's own presence (the unitive way).

While there certainly are people who have reported experiences of the mystical presence of God who have not followed this path in any discernible way, and there are certainly people who report sudden existential experiences of the divine presence who were not even intent upon a spiritual life,[3] the path of intentional spiritual direction emerges with great clarity. As Thomas Merton says, "There are no shortcuts."

> The only trouble is that in the spiritual life there are no tricks and no shortcuts. Those who imagine that they can discover special gimmicks and put them to work for themselves usually ignore God's will and his grace. They are self-confident and even self-complacent. They make up their minds that they are going to attain to this or that, and try to write their own ticket in the life of contemplation. But certain systems of spirituality—notably Zen Buddhism—place great stress on a severe, no-nonsense style of direction that makes short work of this kind of confidence. One cannot begin to face the real difficulties of the life of prayer and meditation unless one is first perfectly content to

be a beginner and really experience himself as one
who knows little or nothing, and has a desperate
need to learn the bare rudiments. Those who think
they "know" from the beginning will never come
to know anything.[4]

I want never to be guilty of doing what I discussed
earlier, trying to put the spirit of God into the "box" of the
three stages of spiritual growth. There is so much wisdom
in what the ancient voices of our faith have said about this
journey that it is very tempting to say that this is "the way,"
but that is not what I am saying. I am saying that the disciplines of our faith, the spiritual exercises that have long
been taught as means of nurturing faith, can all be understood and employed in the light of this path of spiritual
direction. The remainder of this text is devoted to explor-
ing the spiritual journey along the well-marked path of
the ancient saints of our faith.

CHAPTER 4

Purgative

Abba Ammonas was asked, "What is the 'narrow and hard way'?" (Matt. 7:14). He replied, "The 'narrow and hard way' is this, to control your thoughts, and to strip yourself of your own will, for the sake of God. This is also the meaning of the sentence, 'Lo, we have left everything and followed you'" (Matt. 19:27).
Sayings of the Desert Fathers[1]

The first step of the spiritual journey may well be the one that will require the most explanation in our modern age. Christopher Lasch describes our age as one in which a "competitive individualism" has brought us to a "narcissistic preoccupation with the self."[2]

We did not invent greed and self-centeredness in the twentieth century, but we have come a long way toward making it seem "healthy." Among the advances we may want to marvel at that have come into their own in the past century, we may quickly name aviation, medicine, the harnessing of electricity, and the expansion of municipal services in water, sewers, roads, and bridges. I would also add to this list the incredible science of marketing.

We have learned how to appeal to the human desire for self-gratification. We have learned how to package, display, and advertise food, clothing, cars, and personal hygiene products with such efficiency that most of us now can be led about by our senses without ever noticing what is happening to us. The apostle Paul writes a warning to the church in Philippi:

> For many live as enemies of the cross of Christ; I have often told you of them, and now I tell you even with tears. Their end is destruction; their god is the belly; and their glory is in their shame; their minds are set on earthly things (Phil. 3:18–19).

I don't know exactly what Paul was worried about in Philippi in the first century, but I feel that we have found the fulfillment of the time when we have made a god of our belly, our appetites.

We feel it mandatory to live in two-career families and borrow against our future earnings at terrible credit card interest rates to satisfy our every longing for entertainment, fashion, food, and all that seems to rise up as a nameless, dissatisfied urge within us. We no longer even question our greed; we just check to see if we can possibly afford it. The science of marketing has won over the conscience of our age.

More than that, in the phony popularization of psychology, we have labeled all guilt as "neurotic," making ourselves blind to the fact that to fail to feel appropriate guilt can make us even less mentally (not to mention spiritually) healthy. Our cultural narcissism leads us to believe in our own innocence—or at least to vehemently defend our innocence even if we do not really believe in it ourselves. Unwilling to genuinely examine ourselves and our sins, we may attempt to imitate the spirituality of the saints, but it is a thin facade.

A disgruntled church member once told me that he really disliked our use of a prayer of confession in worship.

He explained, "It sounds so negative." Upon further discussion, it became clear that he also did not believe that such phrases as "I confess that I have sinned in thought, word and deed, in what I have done and in what I have left undone" actually applied to him.

We all have enough false humility about us that we would never stand up in public and say, "I'm innocent," but we are also narcissistic enough to be unable to confess any specific sin. Because the language is still a part of the church we may easily say "I'm a sinner," but when we ask a good church member to tell us what her or his sins are, the response will probably be couched in very general terms. "I guess I should be more loving (but frankly, I don't think Job could tolerate what I have to put up with)." "I should probably be more generous with the church (but no harder than our preacher works, I'm probably giving too much as it is)." "I could certainly be a better parent (but God knows that I'm doing the best I can)."

One of the great truths of the spiritual journey is that it is only the unconfessed sin that can hurt us. It is the unacknowledged, the denied and excused aspects of our lives that force us to lie about ourselves to ourselves and to others. The moment we can acknowledge a sin, recovery begins. It is when we are willing to recognize the controlling voice of our appetites that we can begin to say "No" to the musical question "Aren't you hungry?" (for hamburgers, sex, cars, clothes, houses, vacations, whiter teeth...).

When we are willing to recognize our hostility, our resentment, our anger, lust, greed, and self-centeredness, we find the hope for a new way of being. Like Marley's ghost, we have forged a ponderous chain that we wear. Since everyone around us has been busy forging similar chains, it is difficult to know how to live differently. And so we turn to those who have lived outside of the mainstream of our consumer culture—the monks and nuns of the wilderness, the ancient voices of Christian saints who speak to us of qualities of a spiritual life that break the chains of our addictions (especially our addiction to the lie of our own innocence).

It may be said that what first stands between us and God is ourselves. We must be willing to sacrifice the idolatry of ourselves in order to progress. Hence, Kenneth Kirk says that we must undergo a total conversion of perspective:

> We are concerned with wholly conflicting modes of thought—"self-centeredness" and "self-forget-fulness"; "self-centeredness" and "God-centeredness." "God-centeredness" cannot be evolved from self-centeredness; the self-centered soul must undergo conversion to the roots before it can find a new center in God.[3]

Thomas à Kempis mentions this same issue, telling us that we must first let go of our own will (ego?) in order to discover the will of God:

> Take heed to yourself, and stir yourself always to devotion. Admonish yourself, and whatever you do for others, do not forget yourself. You will profit in virtue just so far as you can break your own will and follow the will of God.[4]

"Hi, My Name Is Adam"

Before we allow this crucial stage of the spiritual journey to be lost in too much theological language, let me first take one specific example of purgation under consideration.

Though it is not universally known by people outside of the program, Alcoholics Anonymous is a very spiritually oriented program of recovery for alcoholics. The literature of AA unapologetically describes the process of recovery as being dependent on God (Higher Power). The program is built around the following twelve steps. Notice the movement from confession to action in the steps of recovery:

1. We admitted we were powerless over alcohol—that our lives had become unmanageable.
2. Came to believe that a Power greater than ourselves could restore us to sanity.
3. Made a decision to turn our will and our lives over to the care of God as we understood Him.
4. Made a searching and fearless moral inventory of ourselves.
5. Admitted to God, to ourselves, and to another human being the exact nature of our wrongs.
6. Were entirely ready to have God remove all these defects of character.
7. Humbly asked Him to remove our shortcomings.
8. Made a list of all persons we had harmed, and became willing to make amends to them all.
9. Made direct amends to such people wherever possible, except when to do so would injure them or others.
10. Continued to take personal inventory and when we were wrong promptly admitted it.
11. Sought through prayer and meditation to improve our conscious contact with God as we understood Him, praying only for knowledge of His will for us and the power to carry that out.
12. Having a spiritual awakening as the result of these steps, we tried to carry this message to alcoholics, and to practice these principles in all our affairs.[5]

Much in this program is imitative of the three ways. It begins with a confession of need, a statement of reliance on God alone, and a statement of a willingness to undergo drastic change. The program expects those who follow it to confront themselves "fearlessly," taking an inventory of their transgressions against others and then doing something about them, starting with confession to someone. Then the steps move into forms of action that involve restitution to those harmed and service to other alcoholics. This is not Sunday school chatter; this is how people restore sanity to their lives and halt a rapid march to an early grave!

Each AA meeting begins with a round-table introduction in which each person present identifies herself or himself by her or his first name and the statement "I'm an alcoholic." The general refusal to name our pain or our sins is tantamount to refusing to get better, mentally or spiritually. Among the first truths that all Christians must accept is that for all of us, our last name is Adam. Even though we may not belong in a church basement meeting of Alcoholics Anonymous, each of us could drop the word "alcoholic" and add something equally meaningful. "Hi, my name is Adam (or Eve), and I'm a (hostile jerk, liar, gossip, manipulator, arrogant twit…)."

And so, to progress in the spiritual life, we must be willing to take a fearless, searching look at ourselves, and to be able to rid ourselves of inordinate anger and pride. Only then can we regain control of our lives, which may mean wresting control from our appetites.

Wisdom from the Wilderness

Although it is tempting to think of our particular age as being unique in its narcissism, it seems that in all ages we have had to be assisted in the process of confronting ourselves. We are all familiar with the gospel traditions about Jesus being led into the wilderness for forty days of temptation and self-discovery before he began his public ministry.

There is a strong and important tradition of spiritual self-examination taking place in the wilderness, the desert places where we are totally alone with ourselves and the demons that threaten to own us. Even the forty-year sojourn of the children of Israel in the desert cannot be seen entirely as a form of punishment for their faithlessness. It was their time in the wilderness that transformed runaway slaves from Egypt into the people of God. And so, spiritual seekers throughout the centuries have returned to the desert to pick up the thread of their lost spiritual wisdom.

The wisdom sayings of a group of men and women who lived as hermits in the Alexandrian desert during the third and fourth centuries have long held a great attraction for me. I have found the *Sayings of the Desert Fathers* to be a rich resource for trying to see the way of purgation with new eyes. Our lives are like theirs in very few respects. Our culture and circumstances are totally different, but precisely that may give us permission to hear them in a less threatening way. No one would suggest that we should imitate them in leaving behind family, work, and civilization itself to go weave baskets in the desert, but if we will listen to the fruit of their struggle, we will find their insights to be a great treasure to the church of our day.

Theirs was no self-indulgent monasticism, but a sincere and drastic effort for God. In refusing comfort they sought always to keep their lives focused on the spiritual journey.

> Abba Poemen said of Abba John the Dwarf that he had prayed God to take his passions away from him so that he might become free from care. He went and told an old man this: "I find myself in peace, without an enemy," he said. The old man said to him, "Go, beseech God to stir up warfare so that you may regain the affliction and humility that you used to have, for it is by warfare that the soul makes progress." So he besought God and when warfare came, he no longer prayed that it might be taken away, but said, "Lord, give me strength for the fight."[6]

We unfortunately know very little about the lives of these men and women, and what few things were written down are often accounts of spectacular visions, conversations with demons, and miracles. But of particular importance to us is how they demonstrated the shift from a self-centered way of seeing the world to a God-centered perspective through the avenue of self-denial and spiritual discipline.

The anchorite said to him, "Please will you be so kind as to take me to Abba Poemen." So he brought him to the old man and presented him, saying, "This is a great man, full of charity, who is held in high estimation in his district. I have spoken to him about you, and he has come because he wants to see you." So Abba Poemen received him with joy. They greeted one another and sat down. The visitor began to speak of the Scriptures, of spiritual and of heavenly things. But Abba Poemen turned his face away and answered nothing. Seeing that he did not speak to him, the other went away deeply grieved and said to the brother who had brought him, "I have made this long journey in vain. For I have come to see the old man, and he does not wish to speak to me." Then the brother went inside to Abba Poemen and said to him, "Abba, this great man who has so great a reputation in his own country has come here because of you. Why did you not speak to him?" The old man said, "He is great and speaks of heavenly things and I am lowly and speak of earthly things. If he had spoken of the passions of the soul, I should have replied, but he speaks to me of spiritual things and I know nothing about that." Then the brother came out and said to the visitor, "The old man does not readily speak of the Scriptures, but if anyone consults him about the passions of the soul, he replies." Filled with compunction, the visitor returned to the old man and said to him, "What should I do, Abba, for the passions of the soul master me?" The old man turned toward him and replied joyfully, "This time, you come as you should. Now open your mouth concerning this and I will fill it with good things." Greatly edified, the other said to him, "Truly, this is the right way!" He returned to his own country giving thanks to God that he had been counted worthy to meet so great a saint.[7]

The desert mothers (Ammas) and fathers (Abbas) did not readily speak to anyone. Detachment from society was a primary component of the life they went into the desert to live. Separating themselves from the comfort, company, and distraction of the world, monks and nuns embraced the solitude of silence as their spiritual teacher. While we must find our spiritual path through the modern world of communication, the office, and the freeway, we can learn from the values they embodied in the desert of ancient times.

At least a part of our unwillingness to think admiringly of those who have devoted their lives, full time, without retirement or vacation, to the task of prayer and spiritual progress is part and parcel of our modern resistance to admiring anyone. Consider the nature of our public discourse, our morbid curiosity about the private lives of politicians, athletes, and movie stars. Why does our culture produce tabloid magazines, and such publications as *People* magazine? Why are we more interested in hearing about Bill and Hillary Clinton's marriage woes and financial misdeeds than we are about their considerable academic accomplishments and contributions to social justice?

There is, among us, a desire to level all of society. If we can get the "inside" story about marital unfaithfulness in the life of a famous person, then we no longer have to acknowledge that person as having character or qualities superior to our own. Who are the heroes of our age? Certainly, young people admire certain sports figures, but let us not confuse that with really looking to them to imitate their character! We may admire the beauty of certain TV or movie stars, but we do not want to emulate them.

I believe that we have convinced ourselves that we are all about the same. In our heart of hearts we tell ourselves that "No one is really better than I am," no matter how absurd such thinking may be. There is here a very misleading confusion between having virtues and being virtuous. Every human being is a combination of strengths and weaknesses. None of us is innocent, and yet, to listen to the public dialogue in newspapers, political conversation, and even church speak, it would seem that we are still looking for that "pot of gold at the end of the rainbow" that is the illusion of personal innocence.

In fact, the saints had particular virtues. One person might be very wise but also very hard to get along with (as was often said of Saint Francis of Assisi); another might have great humility but lack certain other virtues.

A good friend of mine and I were once discussing poverty and our Christian response. My friend is an executive with a national benevolence organization, and he was asking me, "In the face of so much poverty, how do we justify having a home so large that we have 'extra' rooms? How do we justify flying to the coast on vacation, eating out in restaurants, and owning two cars?" My answer was that we should not attempt to justify these things. Such persons as Mother Teresa, who lived in poverty, sharing the crusts of the poor, are to be admired because what they are doing is morally superior to what we are doing.

I believe that we need to learn again how to recognize and to extol virtue in others. I am not "just as good as" Mother Teresa. I am not "just as smart as" Hillary Clinton. The minister down the street from me is much more humble than I have ever been, and I would be a better Christian and a better pastor if I could learn to be more like him. That is just a fact of my existence. It is also true that the minister down the street does not take many risks in his preaching or in his writing, and so it is also true that he would be a more effective pastor if he would use his considerable influence by sticking his neck out a bit more and by being less concerned with being so universally well liked. That is, in my opinion, also a fact of his existence. He has both strengths and weaknesses. I do not admire his weaknesses, but for his strengths he is, very honestly, a spiritual hero in my life. I admire him and hope to grow to imitate his virtue.

In the following pages, we will spend time discussing the virtues that were important to ancient traditions of monastic spirituality, not because we are theological historians with "inquiring minds," but because we are modern spiritual seekers, hoping to learn from the experience of those for whom admiration is an appropriate response. If we can import some aspect of their virtue into our modern lives, we will be much richer for having done so.

If we can make the leap to admiration of those long dead, we may also learn the discipline of noticing virtue in those with whom we live and work and worship. The real heroes of our age will probably never be seen on TV, and they are probably not playing professional sports (though they may be, and if they are, they also know that their virtue has nothing to do with their scoring record!).

Detachment

> Abba Moses said, "The man who flees and lives in solitude is like a bunch of grapes ripened by the sun, but he who remains amongst men is like an unripe grape."[8]

The hurried pace of our lives is no accident. By maintaining the "noise" of activity we avoid the discomfort of confronting ourselves. It is of vital importance that we make provisions for a time of coming apart from the distractions of the world. We need to see and hear the truth, about ourselves first, in hopes of seeing and hearing the truth about God. Although the "retreat" to the desert may look like a fleeing from threat, it is actually a very courageous move—not running from the battle but actually charging the front lines. James Fowler describes it this way:

> What the mystics call "detachment" characterizes Stage 5's willingness to let reality speak its word, regardless of the impact of that word on the security or self-esteem of the knower. I speak here of

an intimacy in knowing that celebrates, reverences and attends to the "wisdom" evolved in things as they are, before seeking to modify, control or order them to fit prior categories.[9]

It has been a most noticeable irony that since I have spoken admiringly about monastic life very frequently among small groups of church members, I have quite often heard the accusation that monks and nuns seek the cloister to "escape the world," but when I have invited the same persons to come with me to spend three or four days in silent reflection in a monastery they recoil in horror. We may be able to be indignant about the monastic calling only until we really think about ourselves in the same setting. Solitude is no vacation! As Thomas Merton describes it:

> For that very reason the dimensions of prayer in solitude are those of man's ordinary anguish, his self-searching, his moments of nausea at his own vanity, falsity and capacity for betrayal. Far from establishing one in unassailable narcissistic security, the way of prayer brings us face to face with the sham and indignity of the false self that seeks to live for itself alone and to enjoy the "consolation of prayer" for its own sake.[10]

The goal of this first step in the spiritual journey, that is called the purgative, is to examine ourselves and to be "purged" of the sins and distractions that have kept us separated from God. In order to learn what these things are that blight our growth, we seek some peaceful detachment from distraction. The traditional move toward detachment is inextricably (either figuratively or literally) connected to the desert. Henri Nouwen says:

> Solitude is the furnace of transformation. Without solitude we remain victims of our society and continue to be entangled in the illusions of the false self. Jesus himself entered into this furnace. There

he was tempted with the three compulsions of the world: to be relevant ("turn stones into loaves"), to be spectacular ("throw yourself down"), and to be powerful ("I will give you all these kingdoms").[11]

Those who sought their detachment in the Alexandrian desert were essentially anchorite monks and nuns. That is, they lived a basically solitary life. In the collections of sayings from the desert we see that they sometimes grouped themselves around a venerated teacher, but the instances of their actually forming a monastic community were rare. This form of detachment, and the lack of community it implied, did not last. It was mostly confined to the East, although there was a Western form of anchorite life in the Middle Ages in which some monks and nuns were actually walled into a cell, usually with their coffins, with only a hole in the wall through which to pass food or work materials.

In spite of the relatively rare expression of anchorite hermits, that severe detachment has come to color the view of monasticism among Protestants as well as many Catholics. However, a prominent Christian monk in this century who lived at least part of his life as a hermit, Thomas Merton, says:

> Some men have perhaps become hermits with the thought that sanctity could only be attained by escape from other men. But the only justification for a life of deliberate solitude is the conviction that it will help you to love not only God but also other men. If you go into the desert merely to get away from people you dislike, you will find neither peace nor solitude; you will only isolate yourself with a tribe of devils.[12]

The thought of spending a great deal of solitary time, especially to do so in the midst of silence and reflection and not in a setting of other distractions (e.g., sports, which are often pursued in silence or alone: fishing, backpacking, camping), is not an inviting thought to most of us. However, once that resistance is overcome and the truth about ourselves is no longer so frightening, solitude becomes an attractive asset. Thomas à Kempis advised the beginning sojourner, "If in the beginning you are often in your chamber, and continue there in prayer and holy meditations, it will be afterward a most particular friend, and one of your most special comforts."[13]

It should be noted, however, that solitude alone will not necessarily produce this experience of self-confrontation. As I mentioned previously, there are sports and other activities that leave many people totally undisturbed for days at a time, but that does not mean that they have become reflective in those times. I was amused to discover that when I did conduct a silent retreat for lay people, upon discussion of how we would use our time for intentional self-examination in silence I discovered that each of them had brought a small cache of books and magazines in case they needed some distractions! We hear from antiquity that this is not a modern phenomena:

> Amma Syncletica said, "There are many who live in the mountains and behave as if they were in the town, and they are wasting their time. It is possible to be a solitary in one's mind while living in a crowd, and it is possible for one who is a solitary to live in the crowd of his own thoughts."[14]

The purpose of detachment is not to escape other people but to bring ourselves into focus. The most necessary part of this first step in the spiritual journey is genuine confession. The desert retreat is to help bring us to the ability to make confession real.

In talking with a Benedictine monk, Brother James, about the events that brought him to the monastery, he told me that he had spent most of his adult life running from unhappiness. He had changed jobs, moved from city to city, from one living circumstance to another. At length, he said, "The one thing that I was trying to get away from was the one thing that I took with me wherever I went—me." In the desert, or in the monastery, or in the solitude of our intentional self-examination, we turn and face ourselves.

Community

This thought of the city of God leads on inevitably to St. Augustine, who apprehended far more clearly than did Clement that "the life of the saints is a social one."[15]

It has been pejoratively suggested that detachment is pursued (especially in the monastic tradition) in order to escape people, perhaps because we just can't stand them anymore. It needs to be said at this point that our periods of detachment are not intended to deliver us from human company, but ultimately to bring us into greater community. In the end of the spiritual journey, we will see that the unitive experience is not only an experience of unity with God, but a unity with the community of God. We must never forget that the primary image of the goal of the spiritual life in the teaching of Jesus is "the kingdom of God." Thomas Merton explains it this way:

We do not go into the desert to escape people but to learn how to find them; we do not leave them in order to have nothing more to do with them, but to find out the way to do them the most good. But this is only a secondary end. The one end that includes all others is the love of God.[16]

Merton also gives explicit instruction about the role of community in a successful life of contemplation:

If you regard contemplation principally as a means to escape from the miseries of human life, as a withdrawal from the anguish and the suffering of this struggle for reunion with other men in the charity of Christ, you do not know what contempla-

tion is and you will never find God in your contemplation. For it is precisely in the recovery of
our union with our brothers in Christ that we discover God and know Him, for then His life begins
to penetrate our souls and His love possesses our
faculties and we are able to find out Who He is
from the experience of His mercy, liberating us
from the prison of self-concern.[17]

In his book about community, *The Different Drum*, M.
Scott Peck talks about the spiritual journey in four stages.
He calls the first one "Chaotic, antisocial."[18] This is almost
a prefaith stage, a time when we are disassociated from
God and mostly disassociated from other people. Entering into some kind of meaningful community is a primary
means (I hesitate to say "the means," although we might
come very close to saying so!) of entering into the faith
journey. Thomas Merton speaks of this regarding his own
attraction to religious life:

> Yet, strangely enough, it was on this big factory of
> a campus that the Holy Ghost was waiting to show
> me the light, in His own light. And one of the chief
> means He used, and through which he operated,
> was human friendship.
>
> God has willed that we should all depend on
> one another for our salvation and all strive together
> for our own mutual good and our own common
> salvation. Scripture teaches us that this is especially
> true in the supernatural order, in the doctrine of
> the Mystical Body of Christ, which flows neces-
> sarily from Christian teaching on grace.[19]

Community is an important consideration in the con-
frontation necessary in the purgative way and as a source
of learning and discerning the will of God in the illuminative way; as Merton says, "'God's will' is certainly found
in anything that is required of us in order that we may be
united with one another in love."[20] And ultimately, how-

ever we experience the goal of the spiritual life, it will have something to do with community.

As I have mentioned, the monks and nuns of the Alexandrian tradition were essentially hermits, but their way of life did not last among monastics. Even among the hermits, however, there was a consistent awareness of the their need to continue in devotion to the community celebration of the sacraments. Kenneth Leech says, "The great Christian mystics were insistent that those seeking spiritual progress must not forsake the sacraments, for they knew the dangers of spiritual pride and isolationism when the individual cuts himself off from the common life."[21]

We often hear people say, "I'm spiritual but I'm not religious," or, "I believe in God but I just don't go to church. I don't believe in organized religion." This sentiment, while it may have a certain tone of spiritual superiority, is typically an expression of self-satisfaction that has very little to do with Christianity. None of us was called to be a "lone wolf" in the spiritual life. The church is the community of faith, and persons of faith need to be in the community.

That is not to say that the church is not rife with hypocrisy, political wrangling, and a level of immature pettiness that would embarrass anyone. The church is all of that and more! However, the church is not a haven in a heartless world. It is more like the laboratory where our faith will be tested and challenged. As Erasmus says, "Thus I put up with this church until I see a better one; and she is forced to put up with me until I myself become better."[22]

It is in allowing ourselves to be known by others, in drawing near in friendship and confidence, that we are able to discover our own need for transformation. If we never get involved and always stay in the back pew or, even worse, move from church to church without ever drawing near to the heart of the church's community, then we never gain any depth.

In one of the rare instances of an abba or amma even mentioning community life, Amma Syncletica said:

> If you find yourself in a monastery do not go to
> another place, for that will harm you a great deal.
> Just as the bird who abandons the eggs she was
> sitting on prevents them from hatching, so the
> monk or the nun grows cold and their faith dies,
> when they go from one place to another.[23]

As severe as Benedict's rule seems to be in so many
ways, his sanity and insight was in his awareness of the
vital setting of community for the living out of the ascetic
life. After naming the "instruments" of the monastic life,
he reminds the monks and nuns who follow his rule, "But
the workshop in which we must diligently perform all
these things is the seclusion of the monastery and our stability in the community."[24]

When I began my study of monastic spirituality I was
living in a very small town and I was learning what the
impact of a real loss of privacy was in close community.
Being a minister in a town of only six or seven thousand
people means that you will never leave home without
being recognized. If you drive too fast, lose your temper
in a store, or have a family disagreement (sometimes even
in your own home), it is not a private matter. And in a
small church, the congregation's intimate knowledge of
your life leaves you feeling naked and vulnerable. The first
time that I visited a monastery I was struck by what their
tight quarters must mean to their individuality. We have
heard monastic life criticized as being some kind of an
"escape" from the "real" world, but, in fact, by living in a
monastery they are locked in a closet with the real world.

In the secular world we find ways of insulating ourselves from the people who annoy us. We choose the
church we will attend, and we will go to another one if
something or someone bothers us too much. We can
change neighborhoods, jobs, or even the city where we
live in order to change our social surroundings. A monk is
assigned by the abbot to work in a particular place in the
monastery and to stand in a particular place in choir.

Given choices about such things, we usually group ourselves by common interests, education, age, and so forth. Such considerations are not a part of monastic assignments. If the person next to you in choir sings terribly, groans when he prays, and wheezes when he breathes, you must learn not to allow such idiosyncrasies to become a source of annoyance because you are going to be next to that person for about seven hours a day for an undetermined amount of time! This is more community than most of us have imposed on us in marriage or child-rearing. In the first book that he wrote upon coming to the monastery, *The Seven Storey Mountain*, Thomas Merton writes:

> By this time God had given me enough sense to realize at least obscurely that this is one of the most important aspects of any religious vocation: the first and most elementary test of one's call to the religious life—whether as a Jesuit, Franciscan, Cistercian, or Carthusian—is the willingness to accept life in a community in which everybody is more or less imperfect.[25]

Thomas à Kempis also ties this issue of acceptance to the spiritual journey in an impressive realization for the age in which he wrote. It is very much a part of the agenda of the purgative step to accept imperfection in others so that we can realize imperfection in ourselves and then let go of the issue.

> Study always to be patient in bearing other men's defects, for you have many in yourself that others suffer from you, and if you cannot make yourself be as you would, how may you then look to have another regulated in all things to suit your will. We would gladly have others perfect yet we will not amend our own faults. We desire others to be strictly corrected for their offenses, yet we will not be corrected.[26]

One of the things that we seek to be purged of in this part of the journey is the feeling that we must always judge others or ourselves. We will see in our discussion of humility what a vital aspect this was to the desert tradition. Liberation from judgment gives us the opportunity to see others as valuable. Merton's definition of sainthood is that it is the gift that allows one to not be judgmental of others. "The saints are what they are, not because their sanctity makes them admirable to others, but because the gift of sainthood makes it possible for them to admire everybody else."[27]

While detachment is a vital tool for the process of spiritual growth, it should be clear to us that detachment is not a goal. We do not draw closer to God by becoming more insulated from one another. In fact, the opposite is true. The only solitude we take with us in the journey is ultimately an internal solitude. Merton writes:

> There is no true solitude except interior solitude. And interior solitude is not possible for anyone who does not accept his right place in relation to other men. There is no true peace possible for the man who still imagines that some accident of talent or grace or virtue segregates him from other men and places him above them. Solitude is not separation. God does not give us graces or talents or virtues for ourselves alone. We are members one of another and everything that is given to one member is given for the whole body. I do not wash my feet to make them more beautiful than my face.[28]

We seek solitude to do battle with the "demons" that have inhabited our temple so that we may return to community with some surcease of these afflictions. Henri Nouwen describes the "gentle" deliverance of solitude:

> We enter into solitude first of all to meet our Lord and to be with him and him alone. Our primary

task in solitude, therefore, is not to pay undue attention to the many faces which assail us, but to keep the eyes of our mind and heart on him who is our divine savior. Only in the context of grace can we face our sin; only in the place of healing do we dare to show our wounds; only with a single-minded attention to Christ can we give up our clinging fears and face our own true nature. As we come to realize that it is not we who live, but Christ who lives in us, that he is our true self, we can slowly let our compulsions melt away and begin to experience the freedom of the children of God. And then we can look back with a smile and realize that we aren't even angry or greedy anymore.[29]

Again, the issues of detachment and community in the spiritual journey are not limited to the monastic traditions. However, it is in the monastic communities that many of the tools for the journey have been most closely practiced and given the most reflection. And so we give considerable attention to the wisdom of those who led truly ascetic lives in hopes of translating their wisdom into our situations.

Asceticism

The apostle Paul writes to the church in Corinth, "I punish my body and enslave it"(1 Cor. 9:27a). What he means, of course, is that he has learned the discipline to say no to his appetites so that he is in charge of his decision making. His choice of words was (if it is permissible to say so) most unfortunate, since they prompted so very many instances of drastic self-mutilation. While we must note such excesses with deep regret, we must not let the issue of asceticism be lost in the gory images of masochism practiced in the name of Christ. As Urban Holmes has written, "When Eastern methods were brought to the West the tendency was to go overboard. Cassian reminds us that asceticism is a means to an end and has value only as it opens us to the presence of God."[30]

It also deserves to be said that the tradition of the East also occasionally verged on (if not completely sold out to!) a docetic view of the world in their extremes of asceticism. Certainly Abba Anthony was one who did:

> He also said, "Always have the fear of God before your eyes. Remember him who gives death and life. Hate the world and all that is in it. Hate all peace that comes from the flesh. Renounce this life, so that you may be alive to God. Remember what you have promised God, for it will be required of you on the day of judgment. Suffer hunger, thirst, nakedness, be watchful and sorrowful; weep, and groan in your heart; test yourselves, to see if you are worthy of God; despise the flesh, so that you may preserve your souls."[31]

But we can happily note that the preponderance of the sayings of the desert fathers and mothers reflects more of the awareness of the use of asceticism for the purpose of temperance; as Abba Gregory said, "These three things God requires of all the baptized: right faith in the heart, truth on the tongue, temperance in the body."[32]

Saint Benedict also believed that temperance was essential to the life of the monk and to all Christians, saying, "If we wish to be sheltered in this Kingdom, it can be reached only through our good conduct."[33]

But for the most part we speak of asceticism not as a matter necessary to our salvation but for the sake of liberation from our addictions, so that we can focus our spirits on God. Thomas Merton says, regarding the ascetic life: "The negative elements, solitude, fasting, obedience, penance, renunciation of property and of ambition, are all intended to clear the way so that prayer, meditation and contemplation may fill the space created by the abandonment of other concerns."[34]

Retreat!

Primarily, those of us who live in the secular world can best attempt ascetic exercises by making a retreat.

Again, this is not a modern invention! One could argue that the most effective dimension of the ancient practice of making religious pilgrimages is similar to the goal of making a retreat. Certainly, no one has done more to formalize the use of the spiritual formation retreat than Ignatius of Loyola.

Ignatius was determined to check the growth of the Protestant Reformation, and to do so he established the Society of Jesus, a monastic order that we generally call the "Jesuits." He recruited faithful Catholics into this new order through the use of the Ignatian retreat.

Ignatius wrote a manual for making an extended retreat. In it he explained several methods of purgative reflection and illuminative meditation. Through the use of his retreat model, he hoped to help retreatants clear their minds of distraction so that they could clearly find the will of God for their lives. It was an extended exercise, not merely for the personal satisfaction of the retreatants' spiritual growth, but to ascertain if they had a calling to vocation in the Society of Jesus. As Kenneth Kirk describes the retreat, "Ignatius never intended the 'Spiritual Exercises' to be a method of meditation or a school of prayer. They had one purpose, and one purpose only—'to conquer oneself and regulate one's life, and to avoid coming to a determination through any inordinate affection.'"[35]

Ignatius formalized an approach to asceticism that allowed itself to be adapted to the needs of different individuals. It has been in use for more than four hundred years. The techniques he employs in his manual pertain to the purgative and illuminative stages. He describes the event he has in mind as being four weeks long, but that is not necessarily intended to limit the event to a literal twenty-eight days. The retreat could be either longer or shorter depending on the needs of the retreatant.

The four weeks have more to do with the four subjects he wants to have covered: "the first, which is the consideration and contemplation of sin; the second, the life of our Lord Jesus Christ up to and including Palm Sunday;

the third, the passion of Christ our Lord; and the fourth, the Resurrection and Ascension."[36]

As is clear from his description, the first week covers the materials that relate to the purgative stage, and the remainder are illuminative in nature. However, Ignatius suggests a form of an examination of conscience, both in a general way and regarding a particular sin or defect that the retreatant is trying to extinguish, for use every day, three times a day. It must be remembered that Ignatius was a person who believed that we could work our way into sainthood if only we tried hard enough! His process was intentional, with the specific goal of recruiting men into the Jesuit order.

The making of a four-week Ignatian retreat is still part of Jesuit tradition, and many members of other religious orders also participate in this lengthy experience. However, as the retreat model has become more and more accepted as a real opportunity for laypeople to make progress in their spiritual journey, Jesuits have attempted to adapt the retreat to the needs of laypersons by making opportunities for us to attend four- and seven-day retreats done in an Ignatian style. Certainly, Ignatian or not, the retreat has become a broadly used opportunity for attempting spiritual exercises.

Kenneth Leech advocates the use of the retreat annually in order to practice the tools of asceticism, especially silence:

> To build up inner resources of silence and stillness is one of the central tasks of training in prayer. In a culture which has almost outlawed silence, it is a matter of urgency that Christians create oases, centers in which inner silence can be cultivated. At times, such a search for silence needs to be particularly concentrated, and this is the purpose of retreats. A retreat is a period of silence, lasting usually between one and five days, in which an individual will sever himself from his environment

in order to give himself up more completely to the
will of God. An annual retreat of some kind is probably an essential feature of serious Christian living, and the conducting of retreats is an important
element within spiritual direction. Not all priests
are good retreat conductors, but many are, and
there is a need to draw more individuals into this
growing sphere of work. A retreat is a time of awakening, of new vision and new zest. Hugh Maycock
once described the retreat conductor's role as being to "astonish the soul." Another major part of a
retreat is to allow an individual to relax and to ex-
pand at leisure, to give some creative space in
which to grow.[37]

Asceticism in the monastic tradition has been held at
a level that is basically in tension with secular life; as the
comforts of the secular world have become more common,
monastic life has become less severe. The spiritual virtue
of asceticism is to be able to turn off the demanding voices
of our addiction to food, drink, conversation, comfort, sex,
sleep, materialism, or any other form of self-gratification
that can distract us from the business of being attentive to
God. Healthy spirituality never suggested that God was
impressed or attracted by how we can make ourselves
suffer!

Changes in monastic life in just the last thirty years
demonstrate the way in which monks and nuns gauge the
tension between their own lives and the lives of those
around them in the secular world. At the Cistercian monastery that was home to Thomas Merton, Gethsemani,
monks can now speak to one another much more freely.
Whereas they used to have a bunk in a tiny cubicle only
partially divided from other monks' quarters, they all now
have fairly comfortable rooms in which they can keep some
personal items. Several of the monks whom I know personally even have private hobbies that would have been
unheard of a few years ago, some of which require the

possession of radios, cameras, telescopes, and the like. Still, their lives are not like ours. Merton warns that all who enter the religious life must be willing to accept substantive sacrifice:

> No matter what religious Order a man enters, whether its Rule be easy or strict in itself does not much matter; if his vocation is to be really fruitful it must cost him something, and must be a real sacrifice. It must be a cross, a true renunciation of natural goods, even of the highest natural goods.[38]

I have witnessed times when a monk would graciously receive a gift from a friend or family member, giving every sign that he was delighted with the personal acquisition, only to later give it to the monastery, or the poor, or another visitor. With each acquisition one can hear the debate, "Why would I have this?" "What purpose does it serve?" This sort of self-questioning is so foreign to our consumer culture that it is reason enough to schedule time for a retreat, simply to be in the presence of a spiritually minded individual for whom acquisition and consumption are not primary motives in life.

The brothers at Gethsemani, being located in Kentucky where the summers are often very hot with very high humidity, finally decided to install air conditioning in the monks' quarters—only to decide shortly thereafter to not run the air conditioning and to send the money saved on their electric bill to support the work of Mother Teresa in Calcutta! Comfort is not to be denied for no reason, and neither is it to be pursued without reflection.

When I asked the guestmaster at Gethsemani, Brother Luke, to tell me what the goal of modern monasticism is, his response would not have been considered rare in any other century of the Christian era. He said, "Achieving union with God through the practice of the evangelical counsels: poverty, chastity, obedience, stability, and through them the conversion of one's whole life." As we look closer at the particular struggles and tools of the spiritual journey, we must also hold in tension that the goal is union with God and that each of the forms of asceticism we discuss are valuable only as they assist us in the attainment of that goal.

Silence

Bonum est praestolari cum silentio salutare Dei.
(It is good to wait in silence for the salvation of God.)[39]

Before we can move on to discuss some of the specific battles to be encountered in "the desert," we need to take a serious look at the companion issue of silence. As I have previously noted, it is possible to carry the noise of our lives with us into the wilderness. At first we must risk being alone; then we must risk being genuinely still. As Kenneth Leech has written, "Coming to terms with silence is a necessary element in self-knowledge and in prayer. Pascal claimed that 'most of man's troubles come from his not being able to sit quietly in his chamber.' Throughout the writings of all the great spiritual guides, we find the call to inner silence."[40]

The attainment of inner silence is a matter of active choice. We must elect to close out the various forms of stimulation that normally occupy our thoughts. That is why so much is said regarding simplicity in the spiritual life. Thomas à Kempis also describes the election of silence in his advice in *The Imitation of Christ*:

> O my soul, take heed to what has been said before and shut the doors of your sensuality, which are your five senses, so that you may hear inwardly what our Lord Jesus speaks within your soul. Thus says your beloved: I am your health, I am your peace, I am your life. Keep yourself in Me and you will find peace in Me.[41]

Silence is a resource that is employed in every stage of the spiritual journey. In silence we confront ourselves in the purgative way; in silence we grow in meditation and reflection in the illuminative way; and in silence we learn the activity of contemplation in the unitive way. Thomas Merton, drawing again on the wisdom of the desert tradition, stresses the importance of silence during the entire journey of spiritual growth:

> Whatever one may think of the value of communal celebration with all kinds of song and self-expression—and these certainly have their place—the kind of prayer we here speak of as properly "monastic" (though it may also fit into the life of any lay person who is attracted to it) is a prayer of silence, simplicity, contemplative and meditative unity, a deep personal integration in an attentive, watchful listening of "the heart."
>
> The inseparable unity of silence and monastic prayer was well described by a Syrian monk, Isaac of Niniveh: "Many are avidly seeking but they alone find who remain in continual silence…Every man who delights in a multitude of words, even though he says admirable things, is empty within. If you love truth, be a lover of silence. Silence like the sunlight will illuminate you in God and will deliver you from the phantoms of ignorance. Silence will unite you to God himself…"
>
> More than all things love silence: it brings you a fruit that tongue cannot describe. In the beginning we have to force ourselves to be silent. May God give you an experience of this "something" that is born of silence. If only you practice this, untold light will dawn on you in consequence…after a certain sweetness is born in the heart of this exercise and the body is drawn almost by force to remain in silence.[42]

At times, the desert fathers and mothers will speak of silence as a panacea in the search for God, especially as it relates to the illumination of the soul. "A brother came to Scetis to visit Abba Moses and asked him for a word. The old man said to him, 'Go, sit in your cell, and your cell will teach you everything.'"[43]

In a very direct way, Abba Ammonas instructed Anthony about the illuminative value of silence when he wrote to him:

> Behold, my beloved, I have shown you the power of silence, how thoroughly it heals and how fully pleasing it is to God. Wherefore I have written to you to show yourselves strong in this work you have undertaken, so that you may know that it is by silence that the saints grew, that it was because of silence that the mysteries of God were known to them.[44]

Thomas à Kempis also connects silence with illumination:

> In silence and quietness of heart a devout soul profits much and learns the hidden meaning of Scripture, and finds there many sweet tears of devotion as well, with which every night the soul washes itself mightily from all sin, that it may be the more familiar with God, to the degree that it is separated from the clamorous noise of worldly business.[45]

In our world, since the advent of radio and television, we are rarely without words. Many work environments have a radio on at all times for "background" music, and in our homes we often turn on the television, even when we have no intention of watching it, just for the "noise" or to keep us "company." We are, as Henri Nouwen describes us, a "chatty society."[46] One of our main problems is that in this chatty society, silence has become a fearful thing. For most people, silence creates itchiness and nervousness. Many experience silence not as full and rich, but as empty and hollow. For them silence is like a gaping abyss that can swallow them up. As soon as a minister says during a worship service, "Let us be silent for a few moments," people tend to become restless and preoccupied with only one thought: "When will this be over?"

We have become so accustomed to meaningless small talk that it becomes almost impossible to resist the tendency to continue to fill the air with words that have no particular message to communicate. When I had become accustomed to making silent retreats at a Trappist monastery, I began to notice how new retreatants would talk in a virtual reflex to the sight of another person, even when talking was specifically what we were not to be doing at that time. Having come genuinely to treasure the experience of silence that I had found there, I wrote with dismay in the journal I kept of my early visits to the Abbey of Gethsemani about a man walking with me down the hall to the 3:15 a.m. Vigils service who looked at me and said, "It's early, isn't it?" It is always early at 3:15 in the morning, isn't it? Such a thing did not need to be said, but in any other context this observation would have been greeted with equally inane talk about the weather or what we would be having for breakfast.

Framed by silence, the words we speak frequently appear to be a quite unnecessary interruption. That is why Saint Benedict was so strict in his prescription that new monks should be prevented from continuing in the way of meaningless chatter until they had learned the inherent value of the words they spoke:

> No matter how perfect the disciple, nor how good and pious his speech he rarely should be given permission to speak for: "In much speaking, you shall not escape sin" (Prov. 10:19). The master should speak and teach, the disciple should quietly listen and learn. No matter what must be asked of a superior, it must be done with humility and reverent submission. We always condemn and ban all small talk and jokes; no disciple shall speak such things.[47]

In the desert tradition, speaking was reserved for instruction, and even that was done with great care. Abba Poemen said, "If man remembered that it is written: 'By your words you will be justified and by your words you

will be condemned' (Matt. 12:37), he would choose to remain silent."[48]

Ever aware of the need to avoid passing judgment, the
desert mothers and fathers advocated silence as a method
of avoiding the verbal judgments of gossip; as Abba
Hyperechios said, "It is better to eat meat and drink wine
and not to eat the flesh of one's brethren through slander."[49]

Although silence is much avoided and generally
feared, once embraced by the pilgrim in a genuine search
for God, silence can be entered into enthusiastically. Thomas Merton exudes joy in his description of his first retreat at Gethsemani:

> The embrace of it, the silence! I had entered into a
> solitude that was an impregnable fortress. And the
> silence that enfolded me, spoke to me, and spoke
> louder and more eloquently than any voice, and
> in the middle of that quiet, clean-smelling room,
> with moon pouring its peacefulness in through the
> open window, with the warm night air, I realized
> truly whose house that was, O glorious Mother of
> God![50]

Silence is not kept as severely in the modern monastic
tradition as it was prior to Vatican II. Even Trappists now
affirm the need for a closer sense of community within
their monasteries that requires much more liberty in speech
than was allowed a quarter century ago, but silence is still
vital to the monastic journey. Trying to understand its cur-
rent role in monasticism, I asked the Guestmaster of the
Gethsemani Abbey to describe it for me. This is what
Brother Luke said: "Silence is the Great Teacher. It leads to
prayer and increases awareness of God's presence, en-
abling us to hear his voice. To get down to the basic longing
for God and to get away from the useless chatter that promotes vanity and self-absorption. Silence is courtesy both
to God and our brethren."

Not to be despised or neglected at any stage or point
in our spiritual lives, we continue to preserve opportunities

for silence in order to continue to preserve the vitality of our faith, for "silence guards the inner heat of religious emotions. This inner heat is the life of the Holy Spirit within us. Thus, silence is the discipline by which the inner fire of God is tended and kept alive."[51]

Anger

In discussing the battle with both the internal and external evils of the world, it is difficult to know where to begin. Perhaps the apostle Paul would start with pride. I will begin with something closely akin to it. In chapter 1, I quoted Henri Nouwen's statement that anger and greed are "the two main enemies of the spiritual life."[52] I would add to his testimony that of Thomas Merton, who writes in *New Seeds of Contemplation*, "The most difficult and the most necessary of renunciations: to give up resentment."[53] It may seem to be a strange place to begin a process of self-examination, but it seems to be difficult if not impossible to see our own sins if we cannot first let go of some dimension of our sense of how we have been sinned against. There can be no contemplation in the presence of a soul filled with rage. A wonderful illustration of this comes from Zen tradition:

> One day Tesshu, the famous swordsman and Zen devotee, went to Kokuon and told him triumphantly he believed all that exists is empty, there is no you or me. The master who had listened in silence suddenly snatched up his long tobacco pipe and struck Tesshu's head. The infuriated swordsman would have killed the master there and then, but Kokuon said calmly, "Emptiness is quick to show anger, isn't it?" Forcing a smile, Tesshu left the room. [54]

Certainly, the desert fathers and mothers saw the battle with anger to be as vital as any of the moral priorities that they followed so closely. Abba Agathon is reported to have said, "A man who is angry, even if he were to raise the dead, is not acceptable to God."[55] In language that would come as no surprise to anyone who ever had to really struggle with anger, the desert tradition even speaks of anger as though it were one of the demons that were sometimes visible to monks: "Abba Isidore said, 'One day I went to the market place to sell some small goods; when I saw anger approaching me, I left the things and fled.'"[56]

Though it may not be so simple for most of us to see anger lurking about, we can appreciate Isidore's conscious decision to avoid it. Because anger is essentially a response to fear, we may find ourselves choosing anger as a perceived response of strength when we feel frightened or threatened. Anger may even become a replacement for grief or loneliness, or a defense against the pain of rejection. It is expressed in vengeful sentiments, general hostility, impatience, and even boredom. While the ability to become angry in appropriate settings and circumstances is necessary to life, anger elected in the inappropriate settings just mentioned becomes a great hindrance to the spiritual life.

When I first began the habit of making retreats at a monastery, I discovered two very predictable occurrences on the first day of every retreat. The first was that I would fall on the cot of my cell and go to sleep, even though I have never been one to take naps during the day. Even at night, sleep does not come quickly or easily to me.

The second element of my first day on retreat was a gnawing sense of rage. At that time, I had some very difficult and unresolved conflict in my life. The tension, competitiveness, and drive of day-to-day life kept the lid on this conflict. As I would drive up to the monastery retreat house, I could physically let go of the burden of resentment that I had been carrying. Once free from this exhausting responsibility, even for a brief time, I would fall asleep. Upon awakening, the great barrier to my spiritual journey would be there, waiting for me to do something about it.

In the purgative way, we must learn to let go of the resentments that we have stored up against the world and let go of the inappropriate reserves of anger that we have acquired. Even in the ancient world, this decision to fight against our inappropriate anger was not met with immediate success: "Abba Ammonas said, 'I have spent fourteen years in Scetis asking God night and day to grant me the victory over anger.'"[57] Though Ammonas does not say it, we can almost hear him sigh, "but I do not yet have the victory."

Again, reflecting both the importance of the battle with anger and the inherent value of community, we find this example from the desert of a very intentional victory over anger:

> When Abba Romanos was at the point of death, his disciples gathered round him and said, "How ought we to conduct ourselves?" The old man said to them, "I do not think I have ever told one of you to do something, without first having made the decision not to get angry, if what I said were not done; and so we have lived in peace all our days."[58]

As I mentioned in the beginning of this section, anger and pride are similar subjects. Anger is a great obstacle to a life of prayer and needs to be dealt with. The answer to anger and pride that comes most clearly from the traditions of spirituality is humility. As Thomas à Kempis writes, "Great peace is with the humble man, but in the heart of a proud man are always envy and anger."[59]

Humility

Of all of the qualities sought by the monks and nuns of the desert tradition, none was held in higher regard than humility. There are hundreds of recorded sayings about humility, many of them having to do with the inability of demons to harm a humble person:

> She [Theodora] also said that neither asceticism, nor vigils nor any kind of suffering are able to save, only true humility can do that. There was an an-

chorite who was able to banish the demons; and he asked them, "What makes you go away? Is it fasting?" They replied, "We do not eat or drink." "Is it vigils?" They replied, "We do not sleep." "Is it separation from the world?" "We live in the deserts." "What power sends you away then?" They said, "Nothing can overcome us, but only humility." "Do you see how humility is victorious over the demons?"[60]

Pride, especially in the extreme of narcissism, is self-worship. Humility allows us the liberty of letting go of our idolatry of ourselves in order to grow in worshipful love of God. But there is another point. A great deal of the pretense of pride is a lie. Our insistence on our own innocence or our own importance is often in defense of our guilt and failures. Embracing humility allows us to embrace truth. Thomas Merton said:

> In humility is the greatest freedom. As long as you have to defend the imaginary self that you think is important, you lose your peace of heart. As soon as you compare that shadow with the shadows of other people, you lose all joy, because you have begun to trade in unrealities, and there is no joy in things that do not exist.
>
> As soon as you begin to take yourself seriously and imagine that your virtues are important because they are yours, you become the prisoner of your own vanity and even your best works will blind and deceive you. Then, in order to defend yourself, you will begin to see sins and faults everywhere in the actions of other men. And the more unreasonable importance you attach to yourself and to your own works, the more you will tend to build up your own idea of yourself by condemning other people.[61]

The trap of condemning others in order to defend your own pride is one that the desert fathers and mothers dwelt on a great deal. Many of the stories from the desert have to do with situations in which one of the ammas or abbas was being asked to pass judgment on a sinner. Their refusals took several cleverly symbolic forms, but the outcome was about the same in each: an absolute refusal to pass judgment. Their attitude is depicted very well in this saying attributed to Abba Xanthias: "A dog is better than I am, for he has love and he does not judge."[62]

In later centuries, we see how Bernard connected humility with the will. Humility also involves a choice to change our self-perception that issues in a luring of the will away from the inclination to mindless self-gratification:

> For Bernard free will—which is really free consent—and God's grace meet to bestow a love that produces good fruit in humanity. This begins with humility that begets a sense of our poverty and our dignity as a baptized person, which leads to three steps toward freedom to love God: (1) the absence of compulsion to sin, *libertas a necessitate*; (2) the possibility of choosing, even to sin, *libertas a peccato*; (3) the inability to sin, *posse non peccare*.[63]

In our age of psychological sophistication, we tend to cringe at a great deal of the self-abasing language of spiritual writings about humility. Similarly, some of the language of our older Christian hymns and prayers of confession just seem to go a whole lot too far. We are certainly not perfect, but it doesn't sound too healthy to think of ourselves as worms either! As I said in the section on detachment, this business of thinking of one's self as a worm should not be seen as a goal of the spiritual life; it is just part of the process. In the end, the spiritual journey does not leave us hating ourselves but actually genuinely loving others and ourselves. As Thomas Merton writes:

> The beginning of love is truth, and before He will give us His love, God must cleanse our souls of

the lies that are in them. And the most effective way of detaching us from ourselves is to make us detest ourselves as we have made ourselves by sin, in order that we may love Him reflected in our souls as He has re-made them by His love.

That is the meaning of the contemplative life, and the sense of all the apparently meaningless little rules and observances and fasts and obediences and penances and humiliations and labors that go to make up the routine of existence in a contemplative monastery: they all serve to remind us of what we are and Who God is—that we may get sick of the sight of ourselves and turn to Him: and in the end, we will find Him in ourselves, in our own purified natures which have become the mirror of His tremendous Goodness and of His endless love.[64]

The subject of humility touches on all other subjects related to a temperate life. In humility we will not tend to dominate relationships or conversations. In humility we do not grasp to make material things our own. In humility we do not seek to control circumstances around us to suit our own comfort. In humility we do not assume that we are always right, but we will try to suspend judgment as far as that is possible. The desert mothers and fathers used the quality of humility to describe the nature of their whole lives in the desert. When asked how to obtain humility, Abba Tithoes gave this rather all-encompassing reply: "The way of humility is this: self-control, prayer, and thinking yourself inferior to all creatures."[65]

Abba Natoes offered his instruction in humility in a detailed description of the ascetic life:

Go, and pray God to put compunction in your heart, and give you humility; be aware of your faults; do not judge others but put yourself below everyone; do not be friendly with a boy nor with an heretical friend; put freedom of speech far from you; control your tongue and your belly; drink only a small quantity of wine, and if someone speaks about some topic, do not argue with him but if he is right, say, "Yes"; if he is wrong, say, "You know what you are saying," and do not argue with him about what he has said. That is humility.[66]

Several parables from *Sayings of the Desert Fathers* depict the extent of their practice of humility. Some even describe how an abba helped a robber load the abba's possessions onto the robber's donkey, and how another abba chased down some robbers who had failed to find two gold coins in the abba's cell.

In later monastic tradition, humility played no smaller role. In *The Rule of St. Benedict* we find a lengthy description of the twelve steps a monk should make in humility. The first step ties humility to fear of God in the mode of the "divine fire insurance" we discussed in chapter 2. Benedict says that the monk in pursuit of humility will "constantly remember that those who fear God will find eternal life while those who scorn him will be cast into hell."[67] However, there is a corrective to the use of fear as motivation in the end of the section on humility. When the monk is free of sin and vice, "he will no longer act out of the fear of Hell, but for the love of Christ, out of good habits and with a pleasure derived from virtue."[68] The twelfth step of humility, as Benedict describes it, is:

> when a monk shows humility in his heart and in his appearance and actions. Whether he is in the oratory, at the "work of God," in the monastery or garden, on a trip, in the fields; whether sitting, standing or walking—he must think of his sins, head down, eyes on the ground and imagine he is on trial before God. He must always repeat to himself, "Lord, I a sinner am not worthy to lift my eyes to heaven" (Luke 18:13). And, "I am bowed down and totally humbled" (Ps. 38:8).[69]

A thousand years later, when Ignatius of Loyola would again be giving instruction in humility, we find the language concerning it becoming even more severe and again being connected to eternal punishment. As he begins his instruction for retreatants in that first week of purgation, he invites them to "consider also the innumerable others who have gone to hell for fewer sins than I have committed"[70] and to be "struck with amazement and filled with a growing emotion as I consider how…the earth has not opened and swallowed me up, creating new hells that I might suffer eternal torment in them."[71] And after asking us to compare ourselves (in order to be shocked by how unfavorably we compare) with all other people, the angels, and God, he invites us to see ourselves as "a sore and an abscess from whence have come forth so many sins, so many evils, and the most vile poison"[72]—obviously not a quote that would have ever made it into our feel-good universe of pop psychology!

The goal of all of humility in the spiritual journey is to purge ourselves of the lies about ourselves so that we can be open to the truth about God. Even with the excesses of Ignatius' self-abasement, in the end of the fourth week, the meditations he leads a retreatant in restore a sense of self-worth based on God's love for us:

> Consider how God dwells in His creatures: in the elements, giving them being; in the plants, giving them life; in the animals, giving them sensation; in men, giving them understanding. So He dwells in me, giving me being, life, sensation, and intelligence, and making a temple of me, since He created me in the likeness and image of His Divine Majesty.[73]

Discipline

It was said among the desert fathers that if one of the brothers began to climb up to heaven under his own power that the other brothers should gather together and pull him back down! Certainly an aspect of the humility manifest in all expressions of the monastic life is their dedication to discipline and obedience. The presumption is that the spiritual journey needs guidance and that purely private ecstatic experiences will likely lead one down a destructive path.

The history of religion is full of instances of ecstatic experiences. The common expression of spirituality in early America was in the frontier revival, which included some rather amusing accounts of "holy rolling" (some entranced converts were said to roll for miles through the woods), "treeing Satan" (barking up a tree in the way that a coon dog traps a raccoon or possum), and the "holy shakes" (in which a person is captured in the Spirit and shaken, sometimes for hours). In later years we have witnessed ecstatic speaking in tongues and other inspired physical responses to the presence of the Spirit in the charismatic movement. In both we have witnessed many sudden conversion experiences in which persons attempted to move from the rudiments of a faith journey into a full-blown mystical maturity.

Such pentecostalist expressions have been seen in other places at other times, almost always with a sore need for a disciplined approach to spirituality. Discipline is where the mind sets some parameters for the journey of the heart.

In the midst of a time of an almost anti-intellectual approach to faith, we have Thomas Aquinas to thank for establishing disciplined thought and disciplined life as necessary attributes of the quest for the vision of God:

> But if we take from him [Thomas] two thoughts only—that honest intellectual endeavor (impossible, be it remembered, without moral effort of the highest kind) is no less a service of God than any other, and that ordered discipline is the condition of success in all things, even in the pursuit of the vision of God—and add to them the lesson of his life, that he counted the world well lost if he could

bring those two truths home to men in a time of wild and fanatic imaginations, we shall not think any place too high for him in the roll of Christian heroes.[74]

We may find the charismatic gifts to be very appealing and, like many other endeavors, we would like to move toward maturity much more quickly than the plodding process of personal transformation and tedious education in spiritual matters. While some people progress in the spiritual life much more quickly than others, we must yet realize that there is a lot of distance to be covered between when our crayon colorings are hung with magnets on the refrigerator and when our paintings are hung in the Louvre!

The issue of discipline is similar to our discussion of asceticism in that it involves an ability to say no to our appetites and addictions so that we can make our decisions clearly. Spiritual life has a process. In the illuminative stage we will discuss the need for learning, but clearly, learning calls for a disciplined environment.

The monastic life provides the disciplined schedule that allows the monk or nun to balance work, sleep, study, and prayer. By observance of "hours" for community worship and prayer, the life of the religious is punctuated by the flow of the community into and out of worship. The first hour (Vigils) being at 3:15 a.m. certainly sets an immediate limit to one's addiction to sleep! The whole of the rule sets the pace for the balanced life they seek, so that they all share in the work and share a common devotion to spiritual growth. No one is idle; as Benedict says, "Idleness is an enemy of the soul. Therefore, the brothers should be occupied according to schedule in either manual labor or holy reading."[75]

Meals in the monastic life are taken in silence. Most monasteries have arranged their refectories so that no one is ever sitting across the table facing someone else, and there is the practice of the "lectio" (sacred reading) during meals so that there is meditation instead of conversation. Food in monasteries today is certainly more plentiful than in years past, but there is yet a great deal of discipline in this aspect of life.

It has been very telling to look back on my very first entries in the prayer journal that I kept while at the monasteries I visited. My journal included lots of references to the food, which told a lot more about my addiction to food than it did about the nature of the monastic diet. In recent years many books have appeared in religious bookstores that connect weight control and spirituality. Many of these are a thin veneer of religious language masking a diet book that promotes guilt-ridden or magical thinking (suggesting that God wants you to be thin!). The issue of discipline and food has nothing to do with such vanity regarding appearance. Food can be a distraction, and discipline in the purgative way is to help remove distractions. Eating is stimulation, and so we have tended to desire a diverse and interesting diet in much the same way that we desire a variety of good TV shows. In a monastery, food is healthy and simple. Eating is not entertaining but sustaining.

I once took two other ministers with me for a retreat at Gethsemani. They had never been before, so I showed them around and apprised them of the rules for retreatants there. When I told them when the meals were and that the refectory was closed between meal times, one of the men traveling with me (who was not at all overweight) looked almost panicked. He went into the refectory, found a bag of bread, and stole it! We are not accustomed to having discipline imposed on our appetites.

Postulants who come into a monastery accept the rhythm of the way of life in the community. The establishment of a rule dictates a way of life that gives the whole community a common discipline making it possible for them to live together and for each of them individually to pursue their journey. But the rule is something they share in common and can quote to one another as the standard for their lives. As Benedict says, "Everyone shall follow the Rule as his master. No one should rashly deviate from it."[76]

In the world outside the monastery, discipline becomes all the more important and, sadly, all the more difficult to establish. Most of us who have tried to take prayer and devotional meditation seriously have already tried and failed dozens of times as we have resolved to read the Bible every morning before work, or to spend time alone in prayer every afternoon before going home, or to have a family devotional and prayer time each evening.

Monks live by a set rule (although most monasteries today allow for a great deal of discretion in the living out of that rule). Some churches have tried to impose a schedule of study and prayer on their members; however, most of us in the mainstream church have been left with the impression that we "should" pray and we "should" read the Bible, but we have been given little more than the doomed-to-fail pressure of what we ought to do.

In truth, we are all different, and the discipline that works well for one person may be like an adult trying to wear children's clothing to the next person. For myself, I have found attempting a few minutes of prayer on a daily basis to be very unfruitful. On the other hand, another person might die of boredom in the three- and four-day prayer retreats that I have found to be so rich. But this much I know with certainty: If I do not schedule time for prayer and spiritual nurture, it does not happen. No one will become spiritually mature by accident. John of the Cross warns us, "If you would come to that which you have not, you must go by the way you enjoy not."[77]

Without a disciplined approach to the spiritual life, we will not progress. The concept of having a spiritual director had all but passed from our consciousness until these past few years. It may well be that the recovery of depth in the spiritual life of our churches may be connected to our embrace of the notion of submitting ourselves to some form of disciplined direction in the hows and whens of our prayer and study. Not many pastors are trained in how to give spiritual direction, and many others may feel that they are too busy to give individual members of the church the kind of time that it would take to give someone direction. Still, it is an idea that deserves our serious consideration.

Recognizing the dearth of qualified spiritual directors in our churches, we must turn to other opportunities. Some people may find the resources of inner strength to impose upon themselves a workable schedule of prayer and study. Most of us could profit from making a commitment to a prayer group or a course with scheduled meeting times and assignments that will help us to work with the support and encouragement of others in the class.

For those who live in communities where there is a college religion department, it seems wasteful not to avail ourselves of such educational opportunities. Many colleges offer evening Bible classes that meet only once a week. A couple of semesters of serious college-level Bible study could well change the nature of our biblical understanding more than a lifetime of Sunday school attendance ever could.

When an alcoholic is first trying to stop drinking, the advice given by Alcoholics Anonymous is that he or she attend "ninety meetings in ninety days." It is believed that for the beginner, a weekly AA meeting probably won't be enough. Ninety meetings in ninety days is a disciplined commitment to making a serious start on sobriety. For those of us who have been addicted to our self-indulgence all our lives, some form of disciplined commitment will be necessary for us to make a serious start on a life of spiritual growth. Although I am convinced that it is wrong to dictate any one spiritual "recipe" for everyone, I am equally convinced that whatever disciplined approach we take, it must cost us something in time and energy or it will not work.

Obedience

Per obedientiam homo efficitur idoneus ad videndum Deum. (It is obedience that makes a man fit to see God.)[78]

A major consideration in the area of discipline, and the one that is probably the most hideous to our modern ears, is obedience. In a country that has had the struggle for individual freedom running in its veins since the beginning of the Revolutionary War, and in a modern culture in which traditional authority figures are no longer unassailable and are often even ignorable, the idea of voluntary submission to another's authority does not sound appealing and in some ways does not even sound healthy. In fact, we can think of several examples of very unhealthy blind submission to cult leaders (and perhaps some political leaders), as well as a great wealth of individual examples of passive dependence and codependent relationships in which people fail to be whole human beings on their own. The spiritual virtue of obedience that we hope to understand here is not mindless submission to another, but rather the opposite, a mindful, deliberate decision to live toward a kind and quality of humility that makes it possible for community to exist.

In the tradition of the desert mothers and fathers, obedience was a discipline that freed one of the ravages of one's own ego. Abba Rufus effuses:

> O obedience, salvation of the faithful! O obedience, mother of all the virtues! O obedience, discloser of the kingdom! O obedience opening the heavens, and making men to ascend there from earth! O obedience, food of all the saints, whose milk they have sucked, through you they have become perfect! O obedience, companion of the angels![79]

For them, obedience was the primary door to real humility, to do something that didn't even make sense as a discipline of obedience. The most fascinating example of this is in this story about Abba John:

> It was said of Abba John the Dwarf that he withdrew and lived in the desert at Scetis with an old man of Thebes. His abba, taking a piece of dry

wood, planted it and said to him, "Water it every day with a bottle of water, until it bears fruit." Now the water was so far away that he had to leave in the evening and return the following morning. At the end of three years the wood came to life and bore fruit. Then the old man took some of the fruit and carried it to the church saying to the brethren, "Take and eat the fruit of obedience."[80]

In a more dramatic test, similar to the testing of Abraham, there is a parable about Abba Sisoes, who was approached by a man who wanted to become a monk. Sisoes asked if he had any children. Learning that the man had a son, he told him

"Go and throw him into the river and then you will become a monk." As he went to throw him in, the old man sent a brother in haste to prevent him. The Brother said, "Stop, what are you doing?" But the other said to him, "The abba told me to throw him in." So the brother said, "But afterwards he said do not throw him in." So he left his son and went to find the old man and he became a monk, tested by obedience.[81]

This seemingly mindless obedience is nonsensical in our eyes, but for the desert fathers and mothers it was essential to the kind of humility that they were convinced was the way to the vision of God. Of all of the virtues, humility is most treasured, and obedience is the discipline for obtaining it:

Four monks of Scetis, clothed in skins, came one day to see the great Pambo. Each one revealed the virtue of his neighbor. The first fasted a great deal; the second was poor; the third had acquired great charity; and they said of the fourth that he had lived for twenty-two years in obedience to an old man. Abba Pambo said to them, "I tell you, the virtue of this last one is the greatest. Each of the others has obtained the virtue he wished to acquire; but the last one, retraining his own will, does the will of another. Now it is of such men that the martyrs are made, if they persevere to the end."[82]

In the monastic life, the abbot was obeyed as though the abbot were Jesus Christ. Of course, no one can live in community with another person and be ignorant of the other's failings. The point of such obedience is not to assassinate your brains so that you actually believe that the abbot is like Jesus Christ, but that you decide to obey the abbot in spite of the abbot's deficits. Therein lies the virtue. Benedict advises everyone who reads *The Rule*:

> Listen, my son, and with all your heart hear the principles of your Master. Readily accept and faithfully follow the advice of a loving Father, so that through the labor of obedience you may return to Him from whom you have withdrawn because of the laziness of disobedience. My words are meant for you, whoever you are, who laying aside your own will, take up the all-powerful and righteous arms of obedience to fight under the true King, the Lord Jesus Christ.[83]

In the monastery, the abbot enforces the community's sense of discipline and holds in check any tendency to forget the virtues that they were called to observe. Especially concerning materialism, in the none-too-distant past, the abbot made direct decisions on everything that any monk or nun had in his or her possession. According to Benedict, "The vice of private ownership must be uprooted from the monastery. No one, without the abbot's permission, shall dare give, receive or keep anything—not book, tablet or pen—nothing at all. Monks have neither free will nor free body, but must receive all they need from the abbot."[84]

The degree of the abbot's authority can best be illustrated in Benedict's instructions for how closely the abbot is to maintain the discipline of the community:

> He [the abbot] should verbally reprove the more virtuous and intelligent once or twice; but the stubborn, the proud, the disobedient and the hard-hearted should be punished with whips, even at the first signs of sin. For "the fool is not corrected by words" (Prov. 29:19). And "strike your son with rod and you shall deliver his soul from death" (Prov. 23:14).[85]

Acknowledging the excess of the authority given to the abbot in the ancient culture of the desert, we are left to wonder what shape the issue of obedience should take in the life of the church of our time. Certainly, there is an issue here for consideration in relation to our ecclesial authorities for today. Those of us who belong to theologically free church traditions have been grappling for years with the whole issue of authority and the appropriate role of confessions of faith in the life of our congregations. No caricature of the abuses of authority can rule out the integral role of obedience in the development of the kind of humility that is vital to the purgative way, nor the kind of community that will allow our bishops, regional ministers, district superintendents, or other judicatory authorities to begin again to own their role as teachers and spiritual directors.

Spiritual Director

The first expression of what we would call spiritual direction was in the monastery. Benedict sternly warns the abbots that

> The abbot should always remember that he will be held accountable on Judgment Day for his teaching and the obedience of his charges. The abbot must be led to understand that any lack of good in

his monks will be held as his fault. However, he shall be held innocent in the Lord's judgment if he has done all within his power to overcome the corruptness and disobedience of his monks.[86]

Typical of the earlier desert tradition of avoiding the imposition of monastic life, there was hesitancy to directly supervise another monk, as is indicated in this advice from Abba Poemen:

A brother asked Abba Poemen, "Some brothers live with me; do you want me to be in charge of them?" The old man said to him, "No, just work first and foremost, and if they want to live like you, they will see to it themselves." The brother said to him, "but it is they themselves, Father, who want me to be in charge of them." The old man said to him, "No, be their example, not their legislator."[87]

Urban Holmes traces the beginnings of spiritual direction outside of the monastery to the founding of the Dominican order in the twelfth century:

Preaching was the ostensible task, but they came to be the first to train seriously for spiritual direction. Of course, it had roots in earlier thought and practice. Abelard's (1079–1142) theology had made much of friendship just as did Aelred. Previously the practice of spiritual direction had been in the monastic model, and was generally believed to be needed only by beginners. "Discretion" followed direction. But now, with the Dominicans, spiritual direction was prescribed for everyone. Lay persons were often spiritual guides.[88]

Thomas Merton, in *The Seven Storey Mountain*, bemoans his resistance to real submission to spiritual direction: "Direction was the thing I most needed, and which I was least solicitous to avail myself of. And as far as I remember I only got around to asking Father Moore some trivial questions—what was a scapular, and what was the difference between a breviary and a missal, and where could I get a missal?"[89]

I have discovered only isolated instances of stated, intentional spiritual direction relationships in the Protestant church. It suggests a kind of discipleship that we are unaccustomed to and with which we are possibly very uncomfortable. It remains to be seen if we will avail ourselves of it in this generation.

Sexuality

Before leaving this section on the purgative way, it is appropriate that we consider the relationship between sexuality and spirituality. It has been suggested that the only relationship between spirituality and sexuality is one of war, assuming that sexual desire is always inherently evil. Jesus Christ and the apostle Paul evidently lived celibate lives (though this assumption is vehemently challenged by many biblical scholars). Examples of the desert mothers' and fathers' value of their celibacy abound. One of the stories of Benedict's early life has to with his extinguishing of his lust: "Benedict, responding to the grace of God, Gregory reports, rolled naked in a nettle patch. The pain of the stinging nettles was sufficient to drive out the temptation completely, and never again did he experience another temptation of this kind."[90]

In his book *A History of Christian Spirituality*, Urban Holmes describes how the early movement toward a masculine spirituality was a necessary part of the world's move from antistructure into structure and an action mode. As necessary as this may have seemed at the time to rein in the wanton sexuality of an earlier day, we have paid dearly for it in a loss of the appropriate place of sexuality in spirituality. He writes:

> This is undoubtedly true. It was a hard won victory and the "enemy"—symbolized by the feminine and by sexuality—remained a real threat.

Humanity feared the chaos of living once again under the caprice of passion.

The price we paid for this "victory" was excessive, and through the centuries it took its toll. This survey, with its accounts of ritual castration, deprecation of marriage (if not of women themselves), and repression of orectic forces, will give ample evidence of a compulsive and forced masculine spirituality. The movement from the antistructure to the structure, from the receptive mode to the action mode of consciousness, was necessary and understandable, as much as the results are to be mourned. What we have to do now is reclaim the feminine spirituality and the place of sexuality—even genitality—in the life of prayer, without gainsaying the positive elements in our spiritual heritage drawn from the evolving human consciousness.[91]

Certainly, spirituality has not been purged of sexuality at all times in all places. The presence of The Song of Songs in the Bible is an ancient testimony to an awareness of the appropriate place of sensuality and sexuality in the midst of a spiritual life. Also, it would be hard not to notice the sexual dimension to the language used by both Bonaventure and John of the Cross in their descriptions of the unitive experience of God. In John of the Cross's "Dark Night" he even mixes the pronouns in reference to the two lovers. The pursuer and the pursued are both referred to as masculine and feminine.

Kenneth Leech also advocates a renewal of the place of sexuality in our thinking about our spiritual lives:

Spirituality and sexuality are inseparable. The sexually immature person cannot bypass the quest for sexual integrity in his search for spirituality. If he does, that spirituality will most likely be deranged, and Christian history contains many examples of sexual confusion that finds pseudo-outlets in religious practices. It was on these grounds that Freud came to see all religion as pathological.[92]

As we will explore further in the following chapter in reference to orthodoxy, we can never condemn our bodies and simultaneously draw near to God. Our sexuality can be an affirming aspect of our spirituality. Sadly, however, religion has buried sexuality in guilt, and the secular world has elevated sexual fulfillment to the role of an idol. We need to be as disciplined in our sexual appetite as we are in all other appetites.

Denial of our sexuality is morally wrong and physically and psychologically unhealthy. Equally, wanton irresponsible sexual promiscuity is morally wrong and physically and psychologically unhealthy.

It is not wrong to eat, because eating is necessary to healthy living, but every time you see a billboard with a bacon double cheeseburger on it doesn't mean that you need to go eat one. A spiritually healthy sexuality will involve, again, the descent of the mind into the heart, a marriage of reason and desire.

Application

If it is true that all of us who are on the spiritual journey must pass through this purgative stage, then the resources for the purgative way need to be incorporated into the common life of the church. In the Roman Catholic Church, the sacrament of reconciliation (confession) keeps the issue of the need for self-reflection and surrender constantly before the church. However, many Catholic priests report that fewer and fewer members avail themselves of the confessional. We are indeed a people who resist penitence. However, the opportunity for and the language of confession need to be in the parish worship setting.

In the free church traditions, the absence of a common worship book has led to the decline of the use of corporate prayers of confession and the tradition of including an assurance of pardon in worship. Still, a movement of liturgical renewal has led many individual congregations (lacking the corporate leadership of their denomination) to seek to include genuine personal reflection, examination of conscience, and confession as a part of worship. This trend is to be encouraged.

More than that, it seems that the use of retreats will continue to grow for those who are interested in furthering their spiritual growth. In the context of the retreat we can practice the use of all of the ascetic tools mentioned in this section on purgation, particularly silence and the examination of conscience.

I have also mentioned seeking out a spiritual director, taking classes from a college religion department, or becoming a part of prayer or study group. It may also be helpful, especially in the beginning, to keep a journal of your own thoughts (which may actually be written in the form of prayers of confession).

Through the tools of asceticism, silence, discipline, and obedience we may hope to acquire the humility, the release of our anger, and the recovery of a balanced life in which our appetites no longer make all of the important decisions in our lives. The purgative way is not the goal, but it opens the door to commitment and the opportunity for illumination.

CHAPTER 5

Illuminative

As the old saying goes, "You learn to dance by danc-
ing, you learn to sing by singing," and we will learn to be
spiritual people by putting into practice a spiritual life.
The illuminative way is not simply a way of rote learning.
It is more a putting into practice the insights of a Christian life.

There can be no set amount of time for each of the three
steps of the spiritual journey. The purgative way is very
much dependent upon an individual's willingness to become confessional and her or his willingness to be genuinely humbled and changed. Some people may come to
this point very quickly, while others will only imitate the
language and will never be able to pursue the God who is
beyond their own shadow. In the unitive way, the spiritual pilgrim will eventually reach a point where he or she
must simply wait in openness to God. The vision of God
may come quickly, or it may simply not come. The spiritual journey is not a mechanical one with guaranteed
results.

The purgative and unitive ways may be shorter or
longer, but it is inconceivable that the illuminative way

will be anything but longer. Illumination has a great deal to do with basic learning. Some people certainly learn faster than others, but for everyone there is a great deal of learning to be done. This is one of the real pitfalls of many of the undisciplined approaches to spirituality in which we cast about for an experience that will elevate the spirit into the mystic realms without ever troubling the mind with the tedious task of being exposed to information. As Abba Epiphanius said, "Ignorance of the Scriptures is a precipice and a deep abyss."[1]

Of course, the illuminative way is not just classroom work. The illuminative way involves learning about the faith and learning the practice of meditation and prayer, leading up to the practice of contemplation:

One of the great Carthusians, Guigo II (died c.1193), described the four degrees of exercises of the spirit. The order is very interesting and should be noted carefully. "Seek in reading and you will find in meditation; knock by prayer and it will be opened to you in contemplation." First comes reading, then meditation, then prayer, and finally contemplation.[2]

Essential Learning?

As a minister in a tradition founded on religious tolerance, I am anxious about approaching the subject of orthodoxy, which must be considered in this stage of growth. To say that learning is a vital part of the journey implies that there is something vital that must be learned. Finding agreement about what that something is may be impossible, and indeed the disagreements in this area have led to more than one war. Even the curriculum of a seminary education varies wildly in content. A common joke among seminarians is that the church knows that a seminary education takes three years, but we are extremely uncertain about what we are to do in those three years.

It may be that the process of illumination is also a discipline that must be adhered to for the sake of gaining maturity as much as it is for gaining particular knowledge.

As the philosopher Alan Watts has said, "You do not sing a song to get to the end."[3] A great deal of the value of spiritual reading, religious education, and biblical study is in the shaping of the soul that takes place in the process. The actual information gained in the process may, in fact, be secondary to the transformation that takes place in the individual in the disciplines of the life of a disciple.

Although it would be very difficult for most of us in this age of religious tolerance to come up with a canon of orthodox thought that we would be willing to defend, we can still be in relative agreement that exposure to the articles of faith is a necessary part of the process. We are changed by the process of learning, even if later in the journey we completely abandon much of the specific information learned. As I have said before, God is not in your head. There is no amount of learning that will, like a ladder leaned against the walls of heaven, allow you to ascend into the presence of God. In the end, there is what the mystics call the *via negativa*, the way of unknowing, in which we abandon all knowing in humility before God.

Pseudospirituality will talk about the relativity of all things, and even some of the well-intended short courses in world religions that were so popular a few years ago have led many to assert blandly that they believe in God but in no particular religion. But the truth is that you cannot give up what you have never had. You must, at some point, possess an orthodox faith if you ever hope to transcend it. We memorize the alphabet and read "Dick and Jane" books before we pick up the texts of Søren Kierkegaard's philosophy.

This is also a matter of humility. We all have a tendency to be rather enamored of our own opinions. The only way to come to a realization that our opinions are not necessarily inspired by God is to expose ourselves, over and over, to that which is of God, scripture, and the spiritual wisdom of the saints.

Again, we turn to the wisdom of the ancient monastic traditions to hear of their fervent commitment to scripture:

Abba John, who had been exiled by the Emperor Marcian, said, "We went to Syria one day to see Abba Poemen and we wanted to ask him about purity of heart. But the old man did not know Greek and no interpreter could be found. So, seeing our embarrassment, the old man began to speak Greek, saying, 'The nature of water is soft, that of stone is hard; but if a bottle is hung above the stone, allowing the water to fall drop by drop, it wears away the stone. So it is with the word of God; it is soft and our heart is hard, but the man who hears the word of God often, opens his heart to the fear of God.'"[4]

Two stories from the desert tradition demonstrate their deep concern for orthodoxy. The first concerns Abba Agathon, who was approached one day by some men who were testing him, trying to see if they could make him lose his temper:

"Aren't you that Agathon who is said to be a fornicator and a proud man?" "Yes, it is very true," he answered. They resumed, "Aren't you that Agathon who is always talking nonsense?" "I am." Again they said, "Aren't you Agathon the heretic?" But at that he replied, "I am not a heretic." So they asked him, "Tell us why you accepted everything we cast at you, but repudiated this last insult." He replied, "The first accusations I take to myself, for that is good for my soul. But heresy is separation from God. Now I have no wish to be separated from God."[5]

The second story from the desert about orthodoxy concerns the view of the sacraments. Abba Daniel learned of a monk who led a life that was highly honored in their monastic tradition but who had come to believe that the bread received in communion was not the body of Christ but only a symbol. Deeply disturbed that this thinking was invading their community, Abba Daniel and Abba Arsenius went to visit the errant monk.

They were not able to change his way of thinking in discussion, so they prayed about it and resolved to attend mass together. When they were there in church together, "their eyes were opened and when the bread was placed on the holy table, there appeared as it were a little child to these three alone." As the sacrament was prepared, the three abbas saw an angel descend with a sword and cut the child into pieces. When they went forward to receive the sacrament, the errant monk cried out to God in confession of his faith that the sacrament was the body and blood of Christ, at which time the vision ended and Abba Daniel told him, "God knows human nature and that man cannot eat raw flesh and that is why he has changed his body into bread and his blood into wine, for those who receive it in faith."[6]

This story may seem more than a little strange to Protestant readers. I share it for two reasons. The story is of interest to me in that the brothers went to such lengths to "correct" the beliefs of another monk. In a tradition that revered humility, silence, and detachment as much as theirs did, it is something of a wonder that they would take it upon themselves to tell anyone that he or she was wrong about anything. They almost universally refused to pass judgment of any kind on anyone but themselves. That they enter into this strong debate is an indication of their passion for their understanding of orthodox faith and their willingness to defend it.

Second, I would like to disturb the comfort we feel with our own celebrations of communion in our Protestant churches. A crucial aspect of illumination is our willingness to be changed, to have our thinking and beliefs transformed. However, much of what passes for "Bible study" in our day amounts to little more than pulling the teeth of a tiger. Scripture, when taken seriously, challenges us. It frightens us. It demands something of us. If we read the Bible like a self-help book, looking only for passages that give us comfort, then we had better stay out of the gospels! One critic of the modern church has said that we look like a bunch of atheists with rituals. This is nowhere more true of us than in our observance of communion. This story from the desert fathers brings up the whole matter of making the sacrament something that does not offend us even though it is presented to us as something like an image out of a horror movie.

In the gospel according to John, there is no Last Supper scene comparable to what we find in the synoptic gospels. In John there is a washing of the feet and references to eating, but there are no words of institution, "This is my body," "This is my blood." However, earlier in the narrative, Jesus addresses a gathered throng, saying, "I am the living bread that came down from heaven. Whoever eats of this bread will live forever; and the bread that I will give for the life of the world is my flesh" (Jn. 6:51).

The crowds, quite predictably, reacted with revulsion at what sounded like cannibalism, but Jesus pressed the offense even further, adding,

> "Very truly, I tell you, unless you eat the flesh of the Son of Man and drink his blood, you have no life in you. Those who eat my flesh and drink my blood have eternal life, and I will raise them up on the last day; for my flesh is true food and my blood is true drink. Those who eat my flesh and drink my blood abide in me, and I in them…the one who eats this bread will live forever." (Jn. 6:53-56, 58b)

Even in the text of the gospels, Jesus confronts the disciples for taking offense at this teaching. John records it, knowing that it is gory and offensive and almost impossible to accept. Within the church, we have removed the offense of the crucifixion and made our observance of the sacrament clinical, formal, and clean. We pray for the bread that is "symbolic" of the body of Christ and for the cup that is "symbolic" of Christ's blood. Let me invite you, once again, to get out your concordance and find the biblical passage that describes communion as "symbolic." But don't take a lot of time with this exercise because the word "symbolic" does not appear in the Bible. The New Testament takes a very high view of communion. Why, then, do our churches take such a low view of the sacrament? Let me suggest that at least one reason is that we are attempting to make ourselves comfortable with things that were never intended to be comfortable. Read the apostle Paul's correction of the church in Corinth in their too lax observance of communion in 1 Corinthians 11:17–34!

I do not want to say that I am in agreement with Abba Daniel's view of the Lord's supper, but I can tell you that I am convinced that the sacramental celebration we witness in most of our churches is but a shadow of what is envisioned in scripture. Perhaps it is only a caricature, and that may give us reason to be afraid for ourselves. As we come to a willingness to be open to a path of illumination, we must be willing to allow many of our preconceived notions about faith to die (and sometimes it is a horrible death with lots of tears and fighting).

That Christ is present to us in the sacrament, in the church, that he came to us as a human, is essential to an incarnational view of the Christ. Athanasius argued that the Christ was "humanized" so that we might be "deified." That is, Christ has truly come among us, making it possible for us to find a way to God.

The Illumination of Scripture

One truly universal aspect of the illuminative way, according to virtually all witnesses to the spiritual journey, is the importance of gaining a familiarity with scripture. In early desert monasticism, the reading of scripture was to occupy almost any waking time that a monk was not at work or prayer. As mentioned in the preceding

chapter, in monastic life, the community made use of the
"lectio" so that the communal reading of scripture was a
cornerstone of their daily existence. Urban Holmes says
of monasticism in the middle ages that "the Divine Office
fed the monks, and the Psalter shaped the mind and heart
of the participants."[7] Very much the same can be said of
monastic life today, especially in the Cistercian order where
the chanting of the psalms comprises hours of every day
in the monastery. Consider the amount of actual exposure
we allow in our lives to the content of scripture. Don't do
it during a worship service (the only reason to attend worship is to worship, never to analyze or criticize the service), but using a recording of a worship service from your
church, listen and keep record of how much actual scripture is a part of an hour of worship. How many verses are
actually read aloud?[8] How much of the sermon, the
hymns, the prayers are actually biblical quotes? And if we
are not exposed to much scripture in worship, do we get
it in Sunday school? In the mainstream churches, Sunday
school attendance is typically about one-third of worship
attendance, and most of those in Sunday school classes
are children. Where do we hear the voice of scripture? At
home? In our private reading? In classes we attend?

If we do not allow the voice of scripture to be heard in
our hearts, then we very naturally elevate our own opinions to the level of biblical authority, almost certain that
the opinions we hold are from God or at least tacitly ap-
proved of by God. It is quite possible to be an avid reader
of scripture and still never get the point. It is possible to
read over that which should challenge us and seek out
only texts that confirm our prejudices. Bible study alone
is not going to be the source of our spiritual transformation. However, without a knowledge of scripture there is
no transformation.

Not an IQ Test

"My son is too intelligent to believe in God," a church
member once told me. I had asked her why her college-age

son never came to church. I suspect that she felt that her son needed to be defended and so sought to place him intellectually above those of us who need to believe in God. Nearly dumbstruck, I could only ask, "Is he smarter than Descartes, Anselm, Thomas Aquinas, Kierkegaard?" The fact that her son later went to seminary and is now an ordained pastor is of some considerable comfort to me, but this whole issue of intellect and spirituality deserves some clear conversation.

By way of analogy, let me say that if one person walks up to a water fountain and drinks only a cup of water and is filled, then that person's thirst was only for a cup of water. If another comes and drinks a quart, or even two quarts, that is what that person needed. But behind the water fountain is a system of water pipes, a water tower, and a reservoir holding millions of gallons of water. No person could ever come to the water fountain and drink it all! However, if they are thirsty, they should drink until they are filled.

In the spiritual life, it is as if we have dropped our straw into the Pacific Ocean. We cannot take it all in, but we should all strive to take in as much as we can. Our intellectual capacity is only one facet of who we are. A truly great sermon in one church setting might be heard as drivel in another congregation, and a sermon written for more educated listeners might be totally incomprehensible in the wrong sanctuary. There are legitimate reasons why there are many congregations in every community. My own conviction is that we must all be willing to be challenged so that we are intellectually standing on our tiptoes to try to reach as high as we can. I do not want to read only books that are very easy to understand. In fact, I want to read just above my own level enough so that there are parts of the book that I may not be able to understand at all. We should not seek out only the path of least resistance in our way of illumination.

However, that is not to say that an advanced intellect is spiritually superior to one that is more simple. When, as a graduate student, I began a formal study of spiritual classics, I asked many monks and nuns to tell me which books had had the largest influence on their journeys. I also paid particular attention to the books quoted by the famous Trappist monk Thomas Merton. The list of classics that I distilled from my studies will be obvious to you already: *Sayings of the Desert Fathers*, *The Rule of St. Benedict*, *The Spiritual Exercises of St. Ignatius*, *The Cloud of Unknowing*, *The Imitation of Christ*, and various works by John of the Cross, Bernard, and Teresa of Avila. Believe me, plowing through these works kept me on my tiptoes for several years, and there is much more that I didn't understand there than there is of what I believe that I have digested!

The one author who was not mentioned consistently by a majority of the professional religious I consulted with but who was mentioned too often to ignore was Thérèse of Lisieux or, as she is frequently referred to, "The Little Flower." Thérèse seems to be almost anti-intellectual at times, and yet she was a particular favorite of Thomas Merton, who was about as academic as any spiritual author ever! I mention her in this section on illumination as a possible corrective. Learning is an integral part of the illuminative stage, but that does not mean that unusual theological prowess is so vital that the way is closed to those whose intellectual gifts are not so outstanding. The following is a representative piece of The Little Flower's advocacy for simplicity in thought and her commitment to the role of scripture in illumination:

> Sometimes when I read books in which perfection is put before us as a goal obstructed by a thousand obstacles, my poor little head gets quickly tired. I close the learned treatise that tries my brain and dries up my heart, and I turn to the Sacred Scriptures. Then everything becomes clear: a single thought opens infinite vistas to my soul. Perfection seems easy to me: I see that it is enough to

recognize one's nothingness and to surrender one-self like a child in the arms of God. Leaving to great and lofty souls the beautiful books that I cannot understand, still less put into practice.

I rejoice in my littleness, since only little children and those who are like them will be admitted to the heavenly banquet. Fortunately in the Kingdom of Heaven there are many mansions, for if there were only those whose description and way seem incomprehensible to me, I should never enter there."[9]

E. J. Ross interprets her canonization by the Roman Catholic Church as approval of "a new way of holiness," that of spiritual childhood—simplicity, "littleness," which opens the way to all.[10]

Consider the matter in this way: The way of illumination is necessary not because we have a need for a particular body of knowledge, but because we find our way along a path of orthodoxy that keeps us from straying too far from the path toward union with God. Our journey is not dependent upon great intellect, nor does it ask us to assassinate our brains. The way does not lead, necessarily, down a theologically conservative or liberal train of thought. It seems that growth in Christian maturity will require a relinquishing of the Aristotelian logical notion of noncontradiction, which says that there is only one truth. We are looking for an appreciation of mystery and the humility that will allow us to accept that many of the greatest truths of faith are found in paradox. James Fowler describes this transition very poetically:

The emergence of Stage 5 is something like:
Realizing that the behavior of light requires that it be understood both as a wave phenomenon and as particles of energy.
Discovering that the rational solution or "explanation" of a problem that seemed so elegant

is but a painted canvas covering an intricate, end-lessly intriguing cavern of surprising depth.

Looking at a field of flowers simultaneously through a microscope and a wide-angle lens.

Discovering that a guest, if invited to do so, will generously reveal the treasured wisdom of a lifetime of experience.

Discovering that someone who shares your identity also writes checks, makes deposits and stops payments on your checking account.

Discovering that one's parents are remarkable people not just because they are one's parents.[11]

The way of illumination is not simply about gaining information. It is not so much a matter of becoming knowledgeable as it is a matter of becoming wise. Thérèse of Lisieux may not have been terribly knowledgeable, but she was wise. The spiritual journey is a journey of becoming. In the end, we will not be judged for what we have learned but for who we have learned to be.

A saying from Hassidic Jewish tradition relates, "I did not come to see the maggid [spiritual master] in order to hear him teach Torah but to see how he laced and unlaced his boots." Only a part of the way of illumination has to do with study. The greater part has to do with the practice of faith that changes who we are, right down to the way we lace up our shoes!

Meditation

One of the difficulties in talking about the spiritual journey in a way that makes sense is the fact that the language appropriate to this discussion has been used by so many people in so many different ways that it is often difficult to know what is being said. Nowhere is this confusion more difficult than in trying to discuss meditation, prayer, and contemplation. Many people cannot seem to make any distinction between these three words. In fact, in the spiritual traditions there are drastic differences between them, and there are several identifiable divisions of each (Ignatius, however, does tend to use the word "contemplation" fairly interchangeably with "meditation"). Contemplation is a kind of prayer, but it belongs to the realm of "unknowing" and hence is appropriate to the unitive way. Meditation employs the mind and is generally seen as a preparation to prayer in the ancient traditions.

Meditation is not simply daydreaming, nor is it so specific as doing Bible study. To meditate, we must meditate on or about something. In Protestant tradition, our meditations are most often paragraph-long religious writings—a sort of very short sermon. In Catholic and Eastern traditions, meditation might be more focused on an image, an icon, a statue, or a scene from the life of Christ.

Near contemporaries Francis de Sales and Ignatius of Loyola published very specific directions in methods of meditation. Both of them relied heavily on the use of mental imaging. *The Spiritual Exercises of St. Ignatius*, as previously noted, were written for use in directed retreats for persons who were considering a vocation as a Jesuit. Francis de Sales, in his book *Introduction to the Devout Life*, wrote what he regarded as a simple instruction in meditation for laypersons. The five-step method he prescribed is called the "Salesian method." Urban Holmes summarizes the method in *A History of Christian Spirituality*.

1. Preparation
   (a) Place yourself in the presence of God.
   (b) Pray for assistance.
   (c) Compose the place (i.e., imagine a scene from the life of Jesus).
2. Considerations: identify those images in the scene that affect you.
3. Affections and Resolutions: convert feelings into understanding and then resolutions (acts of the will).
4. Conclusion
   (a) Thanksgiving.

(b) Oblation or offering of the results of the meditation.

(c) Petition to fulfill in your life this day its insights.

5. The Spiritual Nosegay: that which we carry through the day from meditation.[12]

A "nosegay," I learned, was a little bouquet of flowers that men and women carried with them outdoors in the sixteenth century so that the odors from the city's open sewers would not overcome them. The exercise of meditation was to produce some thought that could be carried through the day.

Most of our lives are spent in thinking about something that has already happened or in anticipation of something that may happen. In an age when we seem to be very attracted to diversion, we might also say that we spend a good deal of time just not thinking. Meditation is an activity of thought in the present moment. Meditation is not simple daydreaming, and neither is it intense studying of information. It is a focusing in the present, a kind of mindfulness that is not lost in the distraction of entertainment nor the self-involved considerations of our narcissistic age.

Meditation is not simply the activity of the mind apprehending spiritual ideas. The use of prayers for illumination in both Ignatius' and Francis' meditation methods indicates the reliance upon God's activity of revealing.

Meditation is not dependent upon language but richly incorporates the use of art and mental imaging. Meditation is not necessarily prayer, but it can employ prayer and can be prayerful. In any event, meditation should lead to deeply reflective prayer.

Stations of the Cross

An excellent example of an exercise in meditation is the very old tradition of meditating on the stations of the cross. This exercise combining art, scripture, and written meditations has been in use for about five hundred years. It is most commonly used in the Roman Catholic Church, although many Protestant congregations have begun to appropriate it, especially during the season of Lent.

For the past two and a half centuries, the meditation has included fourteen images or "stations" from the biblical account of the trial of Jesus before Pilate, his scourging, Jesus' carrying his cross from Pilate's house to the place of execution, the crucifixion, and burial. Most Catholic churches have artistic renderings, either in the form of statues or paintings, of the fourteen stations hanging on the walls of their sanctuary. Some monasteries and convents have the stations set up outdoors in a setting of nature.

A person using this meditation exercise may walk from station to station, imagining the events of the crucifixion of Jesus and trying to enter the drama through use of the art, the physical movement from place to place, and by prayer. It is not necessary to take a written devotional guide as you move from station to station, but for persons just starting to meditate in this way, a guide may be of great value. The following series of devotions were written initially for my own use while I was on retreat in a Jesuit community, but it has been used in several Protestant churches during Good Friday prayer vigils in the years since I first composed it.

If your church does not have the stations set up, you can take this book with you to any setting in nature, walk, and then pause to use your imagination as you meditate on each scene as it is described here. For a beginner, it might be easier to visit the sanctuary of a Catholic church and ask to use their stations in the sanctuary for your first attempt at making the stations of the cross. I hope that you find this guide to be fruitful.

First Station:
"Jesus Is Condemned to Death"

Through the many years of Israel's history when they were dominated by other world powers (Assyria, Babylon, Rome), they looked for the coming of God's anointed to deliver them. Their prophecies spoke of a judge who would condemn the wicked and slay those who had persecuted them.

There is no doubt that the masses who followed Jesus did so with this hope. Both in word and deed Christ displayed the power of God. They wanted to make him king, to follow him in battle, to destroy their Gentile oppressors.

It was this hope that brought the crowds into the streets on Palm Sunday. Their hopes were dashed here. The anointed one of God arrived, and when court was convened it was not the Christ sitting in judgment on the wicked, but the wicked holding court to pass sentence on the one who alone is righteous.

He who truly held all power in his hand demonstrates for all the world to see forever that the greatest power is in weakness.

SECOND STATION:
"Our Lord Accepts the Cross"

Here begins the drama that tears our souls apart. How many of us have fantasized about living in those first-century days...actually seeing the Lord himself. How we have longed to touch him, to hear his voice, to draw near to the savior of our souls. Here, the fortunate few, who were born at the right time, are led by circumstances to meet the Lord.

Now they beat with clubs the one we want to embrace, they spit in the face we long to see; brutal fists pound the mouth we desire to hear speak.

We must know that we are also capable of unbridled evil. It is for this evil that we are in such great need of a savior. It is then for me personally that Christ is wounded so that I may be healed. For me that the beaten, thorn-crowned Lord of Glory reaches out and accepts the burden of the cross.

THIRD STATION:
"The First Fall"

Of the fourteen stations of the cross, five are not attested to in scripture. These include the three times the Lord is said to have fallen, his exchange with his mother, and the incident of Veronica wiping his face. Yet the stations all have their place in the traditions of the church from very early times.

The traveler to Jerusalem can follow a street through the city where each of the stations is marked. The location of the first two and the last five are known with relative certainty. The third through the ninth stations take place in a street that was built over the rubble of the city that was destroyed in A.D. 70. This street is then six to ten feet above any street that Jesus would have walked on.

Yet it is not historicity per se that draws us to these devotions. It is an awareness that the drama of the cross did take place. These fourteen stations draw us into the drama; through meditation we become a part of it. We see ourselves as part of the crowd, as a soldier who helps Christ to his feet, as one who jeers or one who wipes his face.

The Lord weakens, falls, draws closer to his death. I walk with him and see myself playing many different parts in this terrible drama.

Fourth Station:
"The Mother Meets the Son"

That Jesus' mother encountered our Lord on the way to his crucifixion is not mentioned in the gospel narratives, but from John's telling of the events we know that she was present at the crucifixion.

It is not at all unlikely that, as this station suggests, the Lord looked up at the angry, jeering crowds and among the faces saw the face of his mother. What thoughts would then have raced through their minds? We can only guess at her feelings. She had heard angels sing at his birth, seen the adoration and hope of shepherds and magi, and heard the prophecy that her own child was to be Israel's salvation. Would she not also have expected to see him become king? Was his miraculous birth and powerful ministry all coming to a culmination in this way?

What mother could stand the visage of her son, beaten almost to death and being tortured by a mob who would surely kill him? Yet, she was not the last to see an innocent son murdered. The world will continue to know the heartbreak, fear, and anguish of Mary until we all have submitted ourselves to her holy child.

FIFTH STATION:
"Simon of Cyrene Is Forced to Help"

Matthew, Mark, and Luke all tell us that a man coming into Jerusalem from Cyrene accidentally ran into the mob and was randomly picked from the crowd to carry the cross for the battered Christ, who could no longer bear the load.

Mark mentions that he was the father of Alexander and Rufus. The fact that he mentions their names would suggest that they are Christians who would have been well known to the early church that first read Mark's writing.

Was it an honor or a burden to be so selected? Unable to stop this fate that Christ also chose to accept, lifting a part of his burden is, perhaps, the most any of us could hope to do.

Each of us is called out of the crowd to bear a kingdom burden, to further the cause of Christ. The coming of the kingdom is achieved as the will of God is done on earth. In the radical acceptance of our calling we lighten the burden of our Lord by shouldering the cross to bear it for a while.

SIXTH STATION:
"Veronica Wipes the Face of Jesus"

Who is Veronica? Where does she come from? Where is the disciple who holds the keys to the Kingdom? Where is the disciple whom Christ loved? Where are those whom Christ healed, or taught, or raised from the dead?

The Son of God cannot see because his eyes are full of sweat, tears, and blood. The one through whom the world was created and is now redeemed presented himself to us in weakness, in need. We are capable of evil, but the visage of the Lord can call out the good that God put in us in the beginning. Perhaps with no prior knowledge of Christ, Veronica steps out of a world gone mad and wipes the face of our Lord.

On the surface her action was a small thing, but it bespeaks a glorious choice: the choice of listening to the voice of compassion, of love, of caring, that cries within our breasts. Like the woman who anointed the Lord before his passion, "she did what she could." I am called to do the same.

SEVENTH STATION:
"He Falls the Second Time"

Although relieved of the burden of the cross, Jesus stumbles and falls again. Some years later the apostle Paul will recount his sorrows in a letter to the church in Corinth. He ends that list saying, "Besides other things, I am under pressure because of my anxiety for all the churches."

Believing in the mysteries of incarnation and atonement, I know that Christ bore daily the burden of his concern for all people, the people of his day and those yet to be born. I look at the man of sorrows there on the pavement. I look at his face and know that I am on his mind. He struggles to his feet and steadies injured knees to stagger forward to the cross for me.

EIGHTH STATION:
"He Meets the Women of Jerusalem"

A crowd of people are following the procession. People in shock, hopes dashed, hearts broken. Some women who can no longer contain their grief begin to wail with sorrow.

Evil is having a heyday. It is to break evil's hold on the world that Christ now goes to Calvary, but even in this event evil will not be removed from the world; the cross begins the long and painful task of bringing in the kingdom. Jesus is the first to suffer for the sake of the coming Kingdom, but he is far from the last to suffer.

He looks now at the weeping women and speaks, in the words of scripture,

> "Daughters of Jerusalem, do not weep for me, but weep for yourselves and for your children. For the days are surely coming when they will say, 'Blessed are the barren , and the wombs that never bore and the breasts that never nursed!' Then, they will say to the mountains: 'Fall on us'; and to the hills: 'Cover us.' For if they do this thing when the wood is green, what will happen when it is dry?" (Lk. 23:28–31)

Indeed, what has happened? The evil in human hearts has pressed beyond the cross to more and more hideous forms of torture and destruction. In earnest we pray, "Your kingdom come. Your will be done, on earth as it is in heaven"(Matt. 6:10).

NINTH STATION:
"The Third Fall"

The way of the cross leads from Pilate's house to the place of execution, a hill just outside one of the city gates. The streets go through what we could call the "downtown" or "business district." The streets are very narrow and are lined with shops and full of vendors.

As Jesus nears the place where he will be crucified, he begins to climb up the hill on the rough stone street and falls again. His human strength is spent. The "lion of Judah" nears his end.

TENTH STATION:
"He Is Stripped of His Garments"

Pilgrims to the Holy Land for the last sixteen hundred years have found the last five stations of the cross inside the Church of the Holy Sepulcher, which was built over the entire hill of Golgotha. Magnificent works of marble, gold, and silver now give honor to him who suffered total humiliation in this place.

The clothing of the one doomed to die belongs to his executioners. Few artists have ever dared to depict the scene that the gospels describe. Jesus Christ, before a crowd of jeering, mocking witnesses, is stripped naked in the midst of a society much more reserved than our own. Pain, grief, and humiliation are heaped upon the one person in all of history who was truly deserving of praise, honor, and admiration.

ELEVENTH STATION: "He Is Nailed to the Cross"

Christ experienced humanity, yet there were many forms of suffering that he did not know. He did not experience old age, divorce, alcoholism, cancer, or a thousand other things we dread in life. The significant thing is that Christ knew human suffering and did not turn from it.

Before he is nailed to the cross, he is offered wine mixed with a drug that would have lessened the pain, but he refuses it. As much as he has already suffered, he chooses to complete this drama experiencing humanity at the point of nails driven mercilessly through his hands and feet.

Thousands of others would have this experience during the Roman occupation of Palestine, but this time when the ringing of the hammer on the nails is silenced, the executioners hear the sound of love in the form of a prayer offered by the condemned: "Father, forgive them, for they do not know what they are doing" (Lk. 23:34, RSV).

In this expression of love, I know that in my myriad sufferings Christ has not abandoned me, but he too is well acquainted with grief and he suffers with me.

TWELFTH STATION: "Death on the Cross"

Jesus hangs on the cross for about three hours before he dies. During the ordeal he speaks seven times: asking forgiveness for those who slay him, quoting Psalm 22, providing for the care of his mother, and offering up his spirit to God. Any of these sayings makes a worthy meditation at this station. But standing here looking up at the image of Christ on the cross, I remember the event in the wilderness experience of the children of Israel.

At one point God's people were plagued with snake bites, and God told Moses to make a bronze snake and place it on a pole. Whenever the people looked up at it they were healed (Num. 21:8). Jesus, like the serpent, is lifted up on a pole to bring healing to all who look upon him.

"And, when I am lifted up from the earth, will draw all people to myself" (Jn. 12:32).

THIRTEENTH STATION:
"His Body Is Taken Down from the Cross"

No mention is made of any of the apostles being present at their Master's funeral. A follower, Joseph of Arimathea, who had previously kept his devotion to Christ a secret, now boldly goes and asks for the body of his Teacher. He is joined by Nicodemus and a few of the women who had followed Jesus as they prepare the body for burial.

Many of the prophets of the day had said that the Messiah would never die, that he would slay the wicked and rule over the righteous forever. Peter evidently put his confidence in these sayings when he refused to hear the Lord's prediction of his death at Caesarea Phillipi (Mk. 8:32).

Feeling the loss of their hope for a restored Davidic kingdom in Israel, most of the disciples are gone, nursing their own grief. These few remain; some, perhaps, assuaging their guilt with lavishly extravagant measures (seventy-five pounds of spices!). But here we see Mary clinging to her grief, soiling her hands and face and clothing clinging to the limp remains of her firstborn. Even when it seems that all hope has died, love remains.

FOURTEENTH STATION:
"His Body Is Placed in the Tomb"

The small funeral procession hurriedly places the body of the Lord in a nearby tomb so that they can return to their homes by sundown. Sabbath is coming, and they do not yet understand their deliverance from the Law.

In many ways it is religion that killed him. It is religion that now tears his mother and these few friends from the tomb where their Savior lay. They are people in bondage: economic and political bondage, religious bondage, and bondage to death. They leave that tomb not knowing that they have planted the seed that will burst forth in three days to end all bondage.

"Very truly, I tell you, unless a grain of wheat falls into the earth and dies, it remains just a single grain; but if it dies, it bears much fruit." (Jn. 12:24, NRSV).

As I have now come to participate in the death of Christ, may I now leave to more fully participate in the life of Christ. Amen.

Prayer

The brethren also asked him [Agathon] "Amongst all good works, which is the virtue which requires the greatest effort?" He answered, "Forgive me, but I think there is no labour greater than that of prayer to God. For every time a man wants to pray, his enemies, the demons, want to prevent him, for they know that it is only by turning him from prayer that they can hinder his journey. Whatever good work a man undertakes, if he perseveres in it, he will attain rest. But prayer is warfare to the last breath."[13]

There are several types of prayer; all of them are difficult. For reasons that will become obvious, I will save our discussion of contemplation for the last chapter of this book. It is the highest form of prayer, but there is none so exalted as to do away with the others. The same may be said of the three movements of the soul. You cannot get to the illuminative way without having been through the purgative, but that does not mean that once in the illumi- native way one ceases to exercise purgation in confession and self-reflection. And those who may manage to enter into a unitive stage of faith will not dismiss books and meditation. Teresa and John of the Cross also affirm this awareness that growth in prayer or the spiritual journey does not imply any bridge burning, but that even the most simple of prayers and all attempts at reading of spiritual books are forms of reaching out to God.

We know of many categories for prayer: confession, illumination, petition, doxology, thanksgiving, interces- sion, and more. For the purpose of this book we can group all of the above together as "vocal" prayer, that is, prayer with a specific subject using very specific language. All vocal prayer is appropriate for beginners.

Prayer is not easy. Whatever kind of prayer we have arrived at the practice of, we need to be conscious of how we prepare to pray. Perhaps one of the most arrogant as- sumptions among modern Christians is that we all just ought to know how to pray. Most of us, including minis- ters and church laity, are amateurs at prayer, and as ama- teurs we need to pay close attention to what we are doing. We need to be very deliberate in how we prepare ourselves for prayer.

Public prayer and private prayer are very different. The prayers we say as a family at the dinner table and the prayers that are said on Sunday morning as the congregation gathers to worship or gathers at the Lord's supper need not dictate the nature and form of the prayers we make in private, which are intended to nurture our relationship with God.

I hesitate to be too prescriptive in talking about how to pray, and yet this subject is far too important to be left with nothing more than the vague suggestion that we should be better at prayer. Let me suggest at least one perspective on how we may approach our growing prayer life: Teresa of Avila describes the degrees of prayer allegorically in the language of watering a garden:

1. Discursive meditation (the use of reason)—watering bucket by bucket, carried by hand from the well.
2. Recollection (affective prayer)—the water wheel.
3. Quiet—springs of water.
4. Union—drenching rain.[14]

When we speak of discursive meditation, the word *discursive* should not be seen as carrying the implication we normally would assign it of being a digression of thought. The sense of it is that in discursive meditation we move from subject to subject intentionally, not haphazardly. Most of our corporate worship prayers are discursive, as well as most of our vocal and mental prayers in private. But here we are talking about discursive meditation as a preparation to prayer.

What Teresa is telling us is that we need to feed our prayer life. If, for example, you plan to spend a few minutes in prayer before going to bed, plan also to spend some time preparing for that prayer time. The obviously helpful preparations may be reading a passage of scripture or a chapter from a devotional or spiritual book. What may be less obvious to us in this age is the importance of the physical aspects of prayer.

Because we believe in the incarnation, the mystical union of the Spirit of God in human flesh, we cannot ignore the fact that we are physical creatures. We can feed our prayer life by being attentive while taking a walk, taking note of clouds, the moon, sun, and stars as well as the faces of those we may encounter while walking. Taking the time to look at art, to consider the architecture of your own house or the tree in your front yard, may help you to make the transition from reflecting about your day at work, worrying about the bills on the desk, the dishes in the sink, the car that needs an oil change, and the phone calls you need to return, and everything else that might hinder your ability to spend a few minutes focused on God alone.

Because we are both spiritual and physical creatures, we cannot ignore even our posture or our physical state at the time of prayer. Don't postpone prayer until you are about to go to sleep. Don't make yourself so comfortable that your thoughts will wander in prayer. Much of the content of this book may be a matter of plowing old ground, but it seems to me that actually finding a place to kneel while in prayer is very helpful. Kneeling is a sign of humility, and it is a posture from which we are not likely to go to sleep or to forget what we are doing.

Walk, read, relax, become focused on our intention of making ourselves present to God, and then, Teresa suggests, we begin to pray by recollection. Recollection refers to the repetition of a verse or sentence of scripture or a memorized prayer. The use of the rosary, the repetition of the Lord's Prayer, or the repeating of any passage of scripture is recollective.

The idea is that most of our attempts at prayer are interrupted by floods of thoughts that become distracting. Rather than trying to force such thoughts out of our minds (which rarely works), we simply attract our minds to a single repeated thought or perhaps a single repeated word. This is also one point where icons and other forms of imaging and religious art can be used to center our thoughts. Because it is so familiar to most of us, simply repeating the Lord's Prayer at the beginning of our time in prayer is an excellent way to call our hearts back into conversation with God.

Teresa then suggests that we be quiet. It is Søren Kierkegaard who says that "Prayer does not change God, but changes him who prays."[15] In our prayers, we are not telling God anything that God does not already know because God already knows everything, including the true content of our hearts. We are not directing God's actions because God is not our puppet to be dispatched by our petitions. Prayer is conversation with God. It is time spent in nurturing our relationship with God. And so, Teresa suggests, we remain silent in the presence of the God who loves us and whom we are trying to learn to love. When that love matures, if we are faithful, there comes the experience that Teresa describes as the drenching rain, the experience of being united with our Creator.

We may very well spend the rest of our lives trying to get this far in our prayer lives. Some, however, will reach a point when a disciplined prayer life that has been rewarding will no longer be so, a time when it seems that faith dies and the spiritual nourishment that had formerly been found in the study of scripture and participation in liturgy will no longer be tolerable. Then, perhaps, these persons have arrived at a crisis that will call for movement into the third way.

CHAPTER 6

Unitive

The process of illumination is, at first, very reassuring. Institutional answers to complex questions about life begin to bring structure to the chaos of living. There is a lot of comfort and security in certainty.

In time, however, the more we learn the more we come to realize that the questions we first asked of faith are much larger than the answers with which we were originally satisfied. We begin to discover contradictions in the doctrines of the church or in scripture. In denial of this feared contradiction, we can find many books in religious bookstores that purport to resolve all of the so-called contradictions in the Bible and other books on apologetics that attempt to remove all doubt from the basic claims of faith. The honest seeker will find very little comfort in such vacuous arguments.

At this point, some people will retreat into an anti-intellectualism that will protect their faith from too much inspection. Others may become disillusioned and lose interest in their faith. Some, however, will dive into the contradiction and emerge into a perspective that is no longer dependent upon the institutional structure of faith

in the illuminative way and that is willing to give up looking for God through the intellect. As Henri Nouwen says
of this stage of faith, "We are on the move from false certainty to true uncertainty."[1]

Some people may be helped through this transition
by having powerful existential experiences of God at an
early point in their journey beyond illumination. We must,
however, regard this kind of mysticism as being very rare.
For most people, the transition from the illuminative way
into the unitive way is experienced with a deep sense of
loss. It is natural that, when a person has found discursive
meditation and a life of vocal prayer to have been very
rewarding, when it becomes dry and unrewarding you
would try all the harder to get back that earlier reward
and confidence of study and prayer. Thomas Merton tries
to prepare persons verging on the unitive way to accept
the loss in openness to the experience that is yet to come:

> And so you will see that in order to cooperate with
> this great work of grace in your soul you must not
> desire or seek the things that God's immense light
> is striving to drive out of you, that He may replace
> them by His own truth. Do not therefore lament
> when your prayer is empty of all precise, rational
> knowledge of God and when you cannot seize Him
> any longer by clear, definite concepts. Do not be
> surprised or alarmed when your will no longer
> finds sweetness or consolation in the things of God
> and when your imagination is darkened and
> thrown into disorder. You are out of your depth;
> your mind and will have been led beyond the bor-
> ders of the natural order and they can no longer
> function as they used to because they are in the
> presence of an object that overwhelms them. This
> is precisely as God wants it to be, for He Himself
> is that object and He is now beginning to infuse
> into the soul His own Light and His own Love in

one general confused experience of mute attraction and peaceful desire.[2]

John of the Cross suggests three criteria for determining if one is ready to progress into the unitive way. He is also concerned that it not be done either too late or too soon. The three signs are as follows:

First, "his realization that he can no longer meditate or reason with the imagination, neither can he take pleasure therein as he was wont to do aforetime." Second, "a realization that he has no desire to fix his meditation or his sense upon other particular objects, exterior or interior." The third and surest sign is "that the soul takes pleasure in being alone and waits with loving attentiveness upon God, without making any particular meditation...without any particular understanding."[3]

The unitive way is closely identified with contemplative prayer, and contemplative prayer, by all accounts, is not an easy thing at which to arrive. Few, if any, readers of this book will likely ever make the decision to leave home and work to pursue a life of monastic prayer or to live as a hermit in constant contemplation. But it deserves to be noted that at this point in the journey we find stern warnings in the writings of spiritual masters about attempting contemplation without direction. The author of *The Cloud of Unknowing* is quite dramatic in her/his warning:

> And now we come to the difference between the contemplative work and its counterfeits such as daydreaming, fantasizing, or subtle reasoning. These originate in a conceited, curious, or romantic mind whereas the blind stirring of love springs from a sincere and humble heart...Some will probably hear about this work and suppose that by their own ingenious efforts they can achieve it. They are likely to strain their mind and imagination unnaturally only to produce a false work that is neither human nor divine. Truly, such a person is

dangerously deceived. And I fear that unless God intervenes with a miracle inspiring him to abandon these practices and humbly seek reliable counsel he will most certainly fall into mental aberrations or some great spiritual evil of the devil's devising...For the love of God, therefore, be careful in this work and never strain your mind or imagination, for truly you will not succeed this way. Leave these faculties at peace.[4]

With a bit less drama but no less seriousness we may add the witness of Thomas Merton:

It is very important to have competent guidance and instruction in the ways of contemplative prayer. Otherwise it will be almost impossible to avoid errors and obstacles. The reason for this is that no matter how good the intentions of the soul may be, its natural coarseness and clumsiness will prevent it from sensing the full import of the delicate work performed by God's love within its most intimate depths and cooperation with His action.[5]

Given the gravity of approaching the unitive stage of faith, we certainly are inclined to seek specific direction in how we are to proceed. As I have previously noted, qualified spiritual directors are few, but let us say that at a bare minimum, no one's spiritual journey should be allowed to take them out of the faith community. Religious fervor can take a person down paths that are not healthy spiritually, physically, or mentally. Some accountability to those around us for the nature and direction of our journey must not be despised.

It may well be that one reason why so few churchgoers ever come to have a very deep spiritual life is specifically because there is very little good direction available. Our experience is of a church that is full of nominally committed Christians, and in many cases a mainline church will harbor one or two people who talk a great deal about spiritual things, who seem to be very committed to a spiritual life, and who are also generally viewed as being most unenviable because they do not seem to be what anyone would want to become. That is to say, as politely as I can, that they are a bit emotionally disturbed. They may talk about what "God has revealed to me" or what the "Holy Spirit has said to me," but in our hearts we are pretty well convinced that neither God nor the Holy Spirit had anything to do with this person's experiences. This is a hard thing to say because, in truth, there were those who thought Jesus was crazy, and many of the prophets were dismissed by their peers as eccentrics.

Just because most of the people who say that God speaks to them are on a spiritual par with the people who tell you that they are Napoleon does not mean that there are not people who actually do hear God speaking. In an earlier chapter, I bemoaned the dearth of recognized spiritual leaders in our churches. This is painfully felt when it comes to having someone to look up to as an example for those who are ready to attempt the development of a contemplative dimension of faith in their lives.

Those fortunate enough to live near a monastery or convent may find a monk or nun who can be helpful at this point. Carefully selected books may also give some guidance. As a final suggestion in this matter, let me remind you of the character of the desert fathers. Be wary of anyone claiming spiritual insight who is argumentative, power hungry, and always seeking recognition. Such negative attributes may not invalidate their own spiritual journey, but they make for poor guides.

Our Work and the Gift of Grace

We come to this vital point at which we long for direction and yet, ironically, there is very little specific advice to be given. M. Scott Peck points out that "Buddha found enlightenment only when he stopped seeking for it—when he let it come to him. On the other hand, who can doubt that enlightenment came to him precisely because he had devoted at least sixteen years of his life to seeking it, sixteen years in preparation?"[6]

This is a very important point. A pseudo-contemplative life might manifest itself in simple indifference. The final step of what is called "infused" contemplation (the experience of being filled with a felt presence of God) comes to an individual by the will and grace of God and not by the voluntary effort of the Christian. Still, preparation is vital. Thomas Merton writes:

> The fact remains that contemplation will not be given to those who willfully remain at a distance from God, who confine their interior life to a few routine exercises of piety and a few external acts of worship and service performed as a matter of duty. Such people are careful to avoid sin. They respect God as a Master. But their heart does not belong to Him. They are not really interested in Him, except in order to insure themselves against losing heaven and going to hell.[7]

As Martin Buber writes in *I and Thou*, "The Thou meets me through grace—it is not found by seeking."[8] It is not that we come to this point only to discover that what we have done until now was wasted effort and valueless exercise. What we have done up to this point has gotten us to this point, otherwise we would not now be faced with this difficult but wonderful opportunity. William James writes of this dilemma in his famous work *Varieties of Religious Experience*:

> "Man's extremity is God's opportunity" is the theological way of putting this fact of the need of self-surrender; whilst the physiological way of stating it would be, "Let one do all in one's power, and one's nervous system will do the rest." Both statements acknowledge the same fact. To state it in terms of our own symbolism: When the new center

of personal energy has been subconsciously incubated so long as to be just ready to open into flower, "hands off" is the only word for us, it must burst forth unaided![9]

What we need at this point is not more ideas, but more openness. In prayer and meditation we focus on an attitude more than a thought. As Merton says:

From these texts we see that in meditation we should not look for a "method" or "system," but cultivate an "attitude," an "outlook": faith, openness, attention, reverence, expectation, supplication, trust, joy. All these finally permeate our being with love in so far as our living faith tells us we are in the presence of God, that we live in Christ, that in the Spirit of God we "see" God our Father without "seeing." We know him in "unknowing." Faith is the bond that unites us to him in the Spirit who gives us light and love.[10]

Ultimately, this "hands off" openness to God will lead us into a discussion of the *via negativa* of contemplation, the way of unknowing. The boundaries between contemplation and where we left off our discussion of prayer by recollection in the chapter on illumination are not terribly firm.

Worship

Certainly one aspect of this phase of the journey continues to be in congruence with all others, and that is presence in worship. As previously mentioned, when Kenneth Kirk sought to sort out the appropriate way to define the goal of the spiritual life, he came to the conclusion that our experience of God must have something to do with our individual disinterestedness (as opposed to panhedonism—that is, seeking God for personal reward). But how do we come to this point of disinterestedness? Kirk offers only one suggestion: worship.

Similarly, Thomas Merton describes the liturgy we experience in worship as being a real vehicle for approaching contemplation. There are two types of contemplation that we see discussed in the literature, "active" and "infused." Infused contemplation is the form of contemplation associated with the mystical experience, but active (still engaging the mind or body) contemplation is a prelude to infused contemplation. And so Merton sees the one leading to the other through worship:

> The liturgy teaches active contemplation above all by its rich content of theology and scriptural revelation, which it surrounds with art and music and poetry of chaste and austere power, deeply affecting to any soul that has not had its taste perverted by the artistic fashions of a degenerate age. But at the same time the liturgy tends to bring the soul to passive or infused contemplation by the power of that great central action, the Mass, in which Christ lives on in the world and in time and by which He draws all things to Himself.
>
> It is in the Mass that we are united to Christ from Whom all the graces of prayer and contemplation flow. Indeed, Jesus is Himself the very embodiment of contemplation—a human nature united in one Person with the infinite Truth and Splendor of God. We become contemplatives to the extent that we participate in Christ's divine Sonship, and that participation is granted to us in a special way in Holy Mass.[11]

The activity of worship can offer introductions to the mystical experience. However, this assumes that our worship services are rich, as Merton says, in theology, scripture, art, music, and poetry. Much of what has been referred to as the "dumbing down" of the church has been a process of evolution from worship as a theologically and artistically profound event toward a consumer-satisfaction driven form of entertainment. Such methods have succeeded in creating several "mega" churches around our country, but I would argue that even though there is a substantial demand for this sort of religious expression, there are yet, and always have been and probably always will be, other religious seekers who want and need something more substantial. A worship experience that includes a theologically and scripturally rich liturgy, profound music, and an intellectually challenging proclamation will also find an audience. These churches, I believe, will still be strong when the faddish super-churches have gone the way of all flesh.

Worship of the right sort may be a preparation to contemplation. If your church has an early service, you may find it possible to attend worship and then, joining with some like-minded seekers, spend the following hour in silence, sitting together in a chapel, attempting to focus yourself in prayer. If there has been content worthy of meditation in worship, you can go to the chapel to allow some single image, thought, or story to center your heart and mind long enough to allow yourself to find the internal silence and stillness necessary to contemplative prayer.

As we approach contemplation, we are trying to set aside the intellectual search for God while continuing to keep our lives faced in God's direction. We are attempting an integration of our mind and our emotion in a way that the Eastern tradition described with the expression, "the mind in the heart." This process is furthered by recollection because this prayer method is dealing with words without particularly dealing with ideas. Henri Nouwen encourages the simple repetition of a centering phrase in prayer:

> John Climacus is even more explicit: "When you pray do not try to express yourself in fancy words, for often it is the simple, repetitious phrases of a little child that our Father in heaven finds most irresistible. Do not strive for verbosity lest your mind be distracted from devotion by a search for words.

One phrase on the lips of the tax collector was enough to win God's mercy; one humble request made with faith was enough to save the good thief. Wordiness in prayer often subjects the mind to fantasy and dissipation; single words of their very nature tend to concentrate the mind. When you find satisfaction or compunction in a certain word of your prayer, stop at that point."

This is a very helpful suggestion for us, people who depend so much on verbal ability. The quiet repetition of a single word can help us to descend with the mind into the heart. The repetition has nothing to do with magic. It is not meant to throw a spell on God or to force him into hearing us. On the contrary, a word or sentence repeated frequently can help us to concentrate, to move to the center, to create an inner stillness and thus to listen to the voice of God. When we simply try to sit silently and wait for God to speak to us, we find ourselves bombarded with endless conflicting thoughts and ideas. But when we use a very simple sentence such as "O God, come to my assistance," or "Jesus, master, have mercy on me, " or a word such as "Lord" or "Jesus," it is easier to let the many distractions pass by without being misled by them. Such a simple, easily repeated prayer can slowly empty out our crowded interior life and create the quiet space where we can dwell with God. It can be like a ladder along which we can descend into the heart and ascend to God.[12]

Beyond all of this repetition in prayer we seek to do a very strange thing. The next step is to try to let go of thought altogether.

Via Negativa

The author of *The Cloud of Unknowing* writes:

A man may know completely and ponder thoroughly every created thing and its works, yes, and God's works, too, but not God himself. Thought cannot comprehend God. And so, I prefer to abandon all I can know, choosing rather to love him whom I cannot know. Though we cannot know him we can love him. By love he may be touched and embraced, never by thought. Of course, we do well at times to ponder God's majesty or kindness for the insight these meditations may bring. But in the real contemplative work you must set all this aside and cover it over with a cloud of forgetting.

It is inevitable that ideas will arise in your mind and try to distract you in a thousand ways. They will question you saying, "What are you looking for, what do you want?" To all of them you must reply, "God alone I seek and desire, only him."

If they ask, "Who is this God?" tell them that he is the God who created you, redeemed you, and brought you to this work. Say to your thoughts, "You are powerless to grasp him. Be still."[13]

Apophatic, or negative, theology is at the very heart of Eastern spiritual thinking. However, the primary text of apophatic theology is from the West. *The Cloud of Unknowing*, quoted above, was originally written in Middle English by a fourteenth-century mystic. The idea of negative theology is not, however, an invention of the Middle Ages. We find it in the theology of the third-century Alexandrian bishop Dionysius, and in the fourth century in the writing of Augustine, who said, "Though we can know that God is, we cannot know what God is."[14] And we find it in the thirteenth-century writing of Eckhart, who said that "nobody is God," and that "to know God one must enter into the darkness of unknowing."[15]

The idea of this way of unknowing is that we must get behind our preconceived notions about God, which may be nothing more than projections of our own ego. When we set out in this journey, we set out to encounter God. At this point we must be willing to let God be God, whoever God is, beyond even the wisest teachings of the saints and our study of spiritually insightful texts.

Here is where *The Cloud of Unknowing* gets its name. In the *via negativa*, having set aside thought, we simply wait in a dark cloud, in a quiet internal emptiness, for God. Reportable results of such an exercise do not come very quickly and are rarely profound. The author of *The Cloud of Unknowing* advises his/her readers:

> And so diligently persevere until you feel joy in it. For in the beginning it is usual to feel nothing but a kind of darkness about your mind, or as it were, a cloud of unknowing. You will seem to know nothing and to feel nothing except a naked intent toward God in the depths of your being. Try as you might, this darkness and this cloud will remain between you and your God. You will feel frustrated, for your mind will be unable to grasp him, and your heart will not relish the delight of his love. But learn to be at home in this darkness. Return to it as often as you can, letting your spirit cry out to him whom you love. For if, in this life, you hope to feel and see God as he is in himself it must be within this darkness and this cloud. But if you strive to fix your love on him forgetting all else, which is the work of contemplation I have urged you to begin, I am confident that God in his goodness will bring you to a deep experience of himself.[16]

As difficult as it is to inspire our churches to be interested in Christian education, it is ironic that at this point in the journey the author of *The Cloud of Unknowing* instructs the pilgrim to avoid even thoughts about God! "I tell you that everything you dwell upon during this work becomes an obstacle to union with God."[17] We cannot chase down and capture God with our intellect, and so the same author advises:

> It is far better to let your mind rest in the aware-
> ness of him in his naked existence and to love and
> praise him for what he is in himself. Now you say,
> "How shall I proceed to think of God as he is in
> himself?" To this I can only reply, "I do not know."
> With this question you bring me to the very dark-
> ness and cloud of unknowing that I want you to
> enter.[18]

Let me illustrate the point we are after here with a brief sketch of the life of the famous spiritual writer Thomas Merton. Merton was born into a Protestant, though not very religious, family. After attempting to find a mean-ingful life in academic pursuits and social justice causes, he felt an attraction to a life of faith. He became a member of a Roman Catholic church, then he took a position as a professor in a Catholic college, and finally he became a Trappist monk.

Early in his life as a monk, he wrote an autobiography. Although it is a well written and very popular text, years later Merton came to be sorry that he had ever published it. As one of his greatest fans, I am also sorry for much of what he wrote in this book because he wrote it before his faith had matured. At the time that he wrote *The Seven Storey Mountain*, Merton was so enthusiastic about his specifically Roman Catholic Christian faith that he said a number of very unfairly critical things about all other expressions of faith. In short, if you read this first book and took it to heart, you would be convinced that only by becoming Catholic (and specifically, by praying to Mary a great deal) could one ever find a real relationship with God.

Years later, Merton died in a tragic accident while he was attending an ecumenical meeting for monastics of all faiths that was being held in a Tibetan monastery. In his maturity, Merton developed close associations with fundamentalist Protestant Christians, Muslims, Buddhists, Jews, and Hindus. However, it is very important to note that even in these relationships, Merton was still very much a Roman Catholic. He never denied his faith heritage, but he rose above the need to make everyone agree with him. He transcended the compulsion to convert, change, and control the faith of other people. He taught, and he could be very inflexible in what he said, but his own intellect and the doctrines he believed in were no longer on an equal footing with God.

For us to enter the cloud of unknowing is not at all the same as denying the truth of what we have come to believe. It is not that our convictions about Christian orthodoxy are wrong. It is that God is greater than our understanding. No matter how much we learn in the illuminative way, we can advance no further than to stand humbly at the threshold of the kingdom and, with heads bowed and eyes cast down, make our request to see God.

Contemplation

The way of unknowing is not the end of contemplation, and yet the goal is not to obtain visions and raptures. The contemplative is someone who is drawn toward God and seeks God for God. To seek God for visions or charismatic experiences is a kind of panhedonism. Infused contemplation is, however, an existential experience of God. Merton defines it as "a supernatural love and knowledge of God, simple and obscure, infused by Him into the summit of the soul, giving it a direct and experiental contact with him."[19]

It seems that there is more of warning than there is of encouragement at this stage of maturity. The via negativa holds out very few enticements. We are accustomed to constant stimulation in our lives, and the practice of silence and detachment begun in the purgative way must be practiced in greater and greater depth in the practice of contemplation. Contemplation involves a great deal of waiting below the "cloud of unknowing" for God to infuse the pilgrim with God's presence. This can be a long wait in a dry desert. Merton cautions those who attempt contemplation:

> Do not think that contemplation, especially in the beginning, brings you a clear, definite knowledge of God. Do not think that your love will always be inflamed to strong, consoling acts that fly to God with great facility. Do not think that your soul will always be lifted up to Him in lightness and liberty and joy.[20]

The author of *The Cloud of Unknowing* tells us what we are to do now:

> This is what you are to do: lift your heart up to the Lord, with a gentle stirring of love desiring him for his own sake and not for his gifts. Center all your attention and desire on him and let this be the sole concern of your mind and heart. Do all in your power to forget everything else, keeping your thoughts and desires free from involvement with any of God's creatures or their affairs whether in general or in particular. Perhaps this will seem like an irresponsible attitude, but I tell you, let them all be; pay no attention to them.[21]

Carved in the stone over the entrance to the Guesthouse at the Abbey of Gethsemani are the words "God alone." The quote is from the founder of their order, Saint Bernard. It refers to this stage of contemplation—when all earthly attachments have been set aside, when our self-idolatry has been destroyed, when we no longer seek God for any kind of reward or security, when we seek God for God alone. How many people have reached this point? How many even would desire such a state? Thomas Merton writes of Bernard:

> Passing beyond all that can be known and understood both spiritually and naturally, the soul will

desire with all desire to come to that *which cannot be known neither can enter into its heart*. And leaving behind all that it experiences and feels both temporally and spiritually and all that it is able to experience in this life, *it will desire with all desire to come to that which surpasses all feeling and experience.*[22]

When the gift of infused contemplation is finally given, the recipient does not feel cheated. Many mystics have tried to explain what their experience has been. Most of their attempts sound like poetry. After dwelling for a considerable time in his own writing, as I have here, on the warnings and pitfalls of apophatic theology, Merton blooms in his description of God's gift through the cloud:

> Then suddenly comes the awakening. The soul one day begins to realize, in a manner completely unexpected and surprising, that in this darkness it has found the living God. It is overwhelmed with the sense that He is there and that His love is surrounding and absorbing it on all sides. At that instant, there is no other important reality but God, infinite Love. Nothing else matters. The darkness remains as dark as ever and yet, somehow, it seems to have become brighter than the brightest day. The soul has entered a new world, a world of rich experience that transcends the level of all natural knowledge and all natural love.
>
> From then on its whole life is transformed. Although externally sufferings and difficulties and labors may be multiplied, the soul's interior life has become completely simple. It consists of one thought, one love: God alone.[23]

Love

Just inside the monastic house at Gethsemani is a sculpture of a very intense-looking monk who is leaning forward holding a banner that reads, "*Amo quia amo.*" Again, the quote is from Bernard: "I love because I love." Thomas Merton explains:

> The great Cistercian theologian of the twelfth century remarks that love is sufficient to itself, is its own end, its own merit, its own reward. It seeks no cause beyond itself and no fruit outside itself. The very act of loving is the greatest reward of love because to love with a pure, disinterested love the God Who is the supreme object of all love can only be the purest and most perfect joy and the greatest of all rewards. Amor praeter se non requirit causam, non fructum: fructus ejus, usus ejus. And he exclaims: "I love simply because I love, and I love in order to love." Amo quia amo, amo ut amem.[24]

The unitive experience of God in contemplation is an experience of love. Ultimately, the spiritual journey is not a journey about visions or sacred wisdom or any other gift. Ultimately, the only thing that matters is love.

> Sanctity and contemplation are only to be found in the purity of love. The truly contemplative soul is not one that has the most exalted visions of the Divine Essence but the one who is most closely united to God in faith and love and allows itself to be absorbed and transformed into Him by the Holy Ghost. To such a soul everything becomes a source and occasion of love.[25]

Finally, then, the unitive experience is an experience of being loved by God, of loving God, and of sharing love with the community. In M. Scott Peck's accounting of the spiritual journey, he describes the final stage with two words: "Mystic, communal."[26] That he uses both words to describe this final stage is very important. The mystical experience, though private in nature, unifies the mystic with the community. Certainly, not all mystics live or lived in communes or monasteries. Most of the mystics of the desert tradition did not. Still, their experience led them to an awareness of their union with others. That is why they would not judge another and why they were committed to generosity and hospitality and to ethical treatment of one another.

Seeds of the insights gained in the purgative way come to flower in the unitive as we realize the truth of what Jürgen Moltmann says: "The nearer we come to Christ, the nearer we come together."[27] The New Testament word *koinonia* is most familiarly translated as *fellowship,* but the same word is also the word translated in the Bible as *communion* and *participation,* and it is the root of our modern word *community.* In seeking to be united to God we are desiring communion, fellowship, and participation in our Creator. As we draw near to God in love, we also find ourselves in proximity to the hosts of others, living and dead, who have traversed the same path. Beyond name recognition and simple courteous familiarity, the spiritual journey necessarily brings us into an intimate loving fellowship of the larger community of faith.

In the unitive experience we discover that the distinctions that formerly gave us reason to be competitive with or to do violence to another human are absurd. Few of us will ever find the strength, commitment, and grace to journey this far, and none of us will be completely at rest until we have. The church waits to reclaim its own wisdom, and God waits for the opportunity to fill us with love.

Notes

Preface

[1]Thomas à Kempis, *The Imitation of Christ*, ed. Harold C. Gardiner, S.J. (Garden City, N.Y.: Doubleday, 1955), p. 32.

Chapter 1: The Nature of the Problem

[1]Kenneth Kirk, *The Vision of God* (Greenwood, S.C.: Attic Press, 1977), p. 69.

[2]Henri Nouwen, *The Way of the Heart* (New York: Ballantine, 1981), p. 58.

[3]Urban Holmes, *A History of Christian Spirituality* (Minneapolis: Seabury, 1980), p. 83.

[4]Leander Keck, *The Church Confident* (Nashville: Abingdon Press, 1993), p. 46.

[5]See, for example, two recent books by theologian John B. Cobb, Jr.: *Becoming a Thinking Christian* (Nashville: Abingdon Press, 1993), and *Lay Theology* (St. Louis: Chalice Press, 1994).

[6]Kenneth Leech, *Soul Friend* (New York: Harper and Row, 1977), p. 90.

[7]Ibid., p. 105.

[8]Thomas Merton, *The Seven Storey Mountain* (New York: Harcourt Brace Jovanovich, 1976), p. 148.

[9]Nouwen, pp. 10–11.

[10]James W. Fowler, *Stages of Faith* (New York: Harper and Row, 1981), p. 183.

[11]Andre Godin, *The Psychological Dynamics of Religious Experience*, trans. Mary Turton (Birmingham, Ala.: Religious Education Press, 1985), pp. 68–69.

[12]Ibid., p. 1.

[13]Holmes, p. 3.

Chapter 2: Where Are We Going?

[1]As quoted in Kenneth Kirk, *The Vision of God* (Greenwood, S.C.: Attic Press, 1977), p. 68.

[2]*The Rule of St. Benedict*, trans. Anthony Meisel and M. L. del Mastro (Garden City, N.Y.: Doubleday, 1975), p. 53.

[3]*The Spiritual Exercises of St. Ignatius*, trans. Anthony Mottola (Garden City, N.Y.: Doubleday, 1964), p. 47.

[4]Ibid., p. 37.

[5]As quoted in Kirk, p. 2.

[6]Thomas à Kempis, *The Imitation of Christ*, ed. Harold C. Gardiner, S.J. (Garden City, N.Y.: Doubleday, 1955), p. 143.

[7]Kirk, p. 2.

[8]Ibid., p. iii.

[9]I use this word, borrowing from Kirk's usage, not to imply a feeling of indifference but rather to stress the absence of greed or any form of self-interest as a spiritual motivation.

[10]Urban Holmes, *A History of Christian Spirituality* (Minneapolis: Seabury, 1980), p. 43, in depicting the approach taken by Augustine.

[11]*Rule of St. Benedict*, p. 9.

[12]Docetism was an early heresy that saw the world divided between a spirit world that was good and a physical world that was evil.

[13]*The Cloud of Unknowing*, ed. William Johnston (Garden City, N.Y.: Doubleday, 1973), p. 50.

[14]Kenneth Leech, *Soul Friend* (New York: Harper and Row, 1977), pp. 150–151.

[15]Kempis, p. 110.

[16]Leech, p. 143.

[17]M. Scott Peck, *The Road Less Traveled* (New York: Simon and Schuster, 1978), p. 269.

[18]Leander Keck, *The Church Confident* (Nashville: Abingdon Press, 1993) p. 31.

[19]G. K. Chesterton, source untraced.

[20]Kirk, pp. 158–159.

[21]Kempis, p. 176.

[22]*The Cloud of Unknowing*, pp. 45–46.

Chapter 3: The Known Steps of The Journey

[1]Urban Holmes, *A History of Christian Spirituality* (Minneapolis: Seabury, 1980), pp. 49–50.

[2]Readers who wish to trace this assertion more comprehensively are invited to review the excellent coverage in either Kenneth Leech's *Soul Friend* (New York: Harper and Row, 1977) or Urban Holmes's *A History of Christian Spirituality*.

[3]We can never ignore such accounts as that of the orphan child, Anna, as told by her adult friend in *Mr. God, This is Anna*, which speaks of a very young child who seemed to possess an undeniable intimacy with God and who spoke with a wisdom to be envied by the most profound of theologians. Also, the research of William James recounted in his landmark text, *Varieties of Religious Experience*, provide ample evidence for the fact that some people, by some inexplicable gift of grace, enjoy profound mystical experiences of God when they are not even seeking a spiritual life. Yet such examples of unsolicited spiritual gifts must be seen as the exceptions that prove that no matter what else may be said or taught about the spiritual life, God is still God and God gives gifts as God chooses (thank God!).

[4]Thomas Merton, *Contemplative Prayer* (Garden City, N.Y.: Doubleday, 1969), p. 37.

Chapter 4: Purgative

[1]*The Sayings of the Desert Fathers*, trans. Benedicta Ward (London and Oxford: Mowbray, 1975), p. 24.

[2]Christopher Lasch, *Culture of Narcissism* (New York: Warner, 1979), p. 21.

[3]Kenneth Kirk, *The Vision of God* (Greenwood, S.C.: Attic Press, 1977), p. 72–73.

[4]Thomas à Kempis, *The Imitation of Christ*, ed. Harold C. Gardiner, S.J. (Garden City, N.Y.: Doubleday, 1955), p. 72.

[5]*Alcoholics Anonymous* (New York: Alcoholics Anonymous World Services, 1976), pp. 59–60.

[6]*The Sayings of the Desert Fathers*, p. 75.

[7]Ibid., pp. 140–141.

[8]Ibid., p. 118.

[9]James W. Fowler, *Stages of Faith* (New York: Harper and Row, 1981), p. 185.

[10]Thomas Merton, *Contemplative Prayer* (Garden City, N.Y.: Doubleday, 1969), p. 24.

[11]Henri Nouwen, *The Way of the Heart* (New York: Ballentine, 1981), p. 13.

[12]Thomas Merton, *New Seeds of Contemplation* (New York: New Directions, 1961), p. 52.

[13]Kempis, p. 57.

[14]*The Sayings of the Desert Fathers*, p. 196.

[15]Kirk, p. 133.

[16]Merton, *New Seeds of Contemplation*, p. 80.

[17]Ibid., p. 78.

[18]M. Scott Peck, *The Different Drum* (New York: Simon and Schuster, 1987), p. 188.

[19]Thomas Merton, *The Seven Storey Mountain* (New York: Harcourt Brace Jovanovich, 1976), pp. 177–178.

[20]Merton, *New Seeds of Contemplation*, p. 76.

[21]Kenneth Leech, *Soul Friend* (New York: Harper and Row, 1977), p. 121.

[22]Source untraced.

[23]*The Sayings of the Desert Fathers*, p. 194.

[24]*The Rule of St. Benedict*, trans. Anthony Meisel and M. L. del Mastro (Garden City, N.Y.: Doubleday, 1975), p. 54.

[25]Merton, *The Seven Storey Mountain*, p. 381.

[26]Kempis, p. 49.

[27]Merton, *New Seeds of Contemplation*, p. 57.

[28]Ibid., p. 56.

[29]Nouwen, p. 17.

[30]Urban Holmes, *A History of Christian Spirituality* (Minneapolis: Seabury, 1980), p. 46.

[31]*The Sayings of the Desert Fathers*, pp. 6–7.

[32]Ibid., p. 38.

[33]*The Rule of St. Benedict*, p. 44.

[34]Merton, *Contemplative Prayer*, p. 19.

[35]Kirk, p. 164.

[36]*The Spiritual Exercises of St. Ignatius*, trans. Anthony Mottola (Garden City, N.Y.: Doubleday, 1964), p. 38.

[37]Leech, p. 180.

[38]Merton, *The Seven Storey Mountain*, p. 292.

[39]Merton, *New Seeds of Contemplation*, p. 46.

[40]Leech, p. 179.

[41]Kempis, p. 103.

[42]Merton, *Contemplative Prayer*, pp. 29–30.

[43]*The Sayings of the Desert Fathers*, p. 118.

[44]Merton, *Contemplative Prayer*, p. 42.

[45]Kempis, p. 57.

[46]Nouwen, p. 43.

[47]*The Rule of St. Benedict*, p. 56.

[48]*The Sayings of the Desert Fathers*, p. 145.

[49]Ibid., p. 200.

[50]Merton, *The Seven Storey Mountain*, p. 321.

[51]Nouwen, p. 37.

[52]Ibid., p. 11.

[53]Merton, *New Seeds of Contemplation*, p. 108.

[54]*Stories of the Spirit, Stories of the Heart* (San Francisco: Harper San Francisco, 1991), p. 297.

[55]*The Sayings of the Desert Fathers*, p. 20.

[56]Ibid., p. 83.

[57]Ibid., p. 2.

[58]Ibid., p. 177.

[59]Kempis, p. 39.

[60]*The Sayings of the Desert Fathers*, p. 72.

[61]Merton, *New Seeds of Contemplation*, pp. 67–68.
[62]*The Sayings of the Desert Fathers*, p. 134.
[63]Holmes, p. 55.
[64]Merton, *The Seven Storey Mountain*, p. 372.
[65]*The Sayings of the Desert Fathers*, p. 198.
[66]Ibid., p. 122.
[67]*The Rule of St. Benedict*, p. 57.
[68]Ibid., p. 61.
[69]Ibid.
[70]*The Spiritual Exercises of St. Ignatius*, p. 56.
[71]Ibid.
[72]Ibid., p. 57.
[73]Ibid., p. 104.
[74]Kirk, p.160.
[75]*The Rule of St. Benedict*, p. 86.
[76]Ibid., p. 51.
[77]John of the Cross, source untraced.
[78]Thomas Merton, *What is Contemplation?* (Springfield, Ill.: Templegate, 1981), p. 24.
[79]*The Sayings of the Desert Fathers*, p. 177.
[80]Ibid., p. 73.
[81]Ibid., p. 79.
[82]Ibid., p. 165.
[83]*The Rule of St. Benedict*, p. 43.
[84]Ibid., p. 76.
[85]Ibid.
[86]Ibid., p. 48.
[87]*The Sayings of the Desert Fathers*, pp. 160–61.
[88]Holmes, p. 68.
[89]Merton, *The Seven Storey Mountain*, p. 323.
[90]*The Rule of St. Benedict*, p. 26.
[91]Holmes, p. 8.
[92]Leech, p. 115.

Chapter 5: Illuminative

[1]*The Sayings of the Desert Fathers*, trans. Benedicta Ward, (London and Oxford: Mowbray, 1975), p. 49.
[2]Urban Holmes, *A History of Christian Spirituality* (Minneapolis: Seabury, 1980), p. 54.
[3]Source untraced.
[4]*The Sayings of the Desert Fathers*, p. 162.
[5]Ibid., p. 18.
[6]Ibid., p. 45.
[7]Holmes, p. 51.
[8]Bear in mind, as Leander Keck has said, that much of the reading of scripture in worship seems almost to dare God to do something! Scripture should always be read well, deliberately, and with a recognition of its importance to us all.
[9]M. M. Philipon, O.P., *The Message of Thérèse of Lisieux*, trans. E. J. Ross (Westminster, Md.: The Newman Press, 1950), p. 24.
[10]Ibid.
[11]James W. Fowler, *Stages of Faith* (New York: Harper and Row, 1981), pp. 184–185.
[12]Holmes, p. 106.

[13]*The Sayings of the Desert Fathers*, pp. 18–19.

[14]Holmes, p. 98.

[15]Kierkegaard, source untraced.

Chapter 6: Unitive

[1]Nouwen, source untraced.

[2]Thomas Merton, *What Is Contemplation?* (Springfield, Ill.: Templegate, 1981), pp. 59–60.

[3]Kenneth Leech, *Soul Friend* (New York: Harper and Row, 1977), p. 163.

[4]*The Cloud of Unknowing*, ed. William Johnston (Garden City, N.Y.: Doubleday, 1973), p. 52.

[5]Merton, *What Is Contemplation?*, p. 55.

[6]M. Scott Peck, *The Road Less Traveled* (New York: Simon and Schuster, 1978), p. 308.

[7]Merton,*What Is Contemplation?*, p. 12.

[8]Martin Buber, *I and Thou*, trans. Ronald Gregor Smith (New York: Scribners, 1958), p. 11.

[9]William James, *Varieties of Religious Experience* (New York: New American, 1958), p. 172.

[10]Thomas Merton, *Contemplative Prayer* (Garden City, N.Y.: Doubleday, 1969), p. 34.

[11]Merton, *What Is Contemplation?*, pp. 29–30.

[12]Henri Nouwen, *The Way of the Heart* (New York: Ballentine, 1981), pp. 64–65.

[13]*The Cloud of Unknowing*, pp. 54–55.

[14]Urban Holmes, *A History of Christian Spirituality* (Minneapolis: Seabury, 1980), p. 72.

[15]source untraced.

[16]*The Cloud of Unknowing*, pp. 48–49.

[17]Ibid., p. 54.

[18]Ibid.

[19]Merton, *What Is Contemplation?*, p. 36.

[20]Ibid., pp. 40–41.

[21]*The Cloud of Unknowing*, p. 48.

[22]Merton, *What Is Contemplation?*, pp. 61–62. The italicized words are quoted from Bernard.

[23]Ibid., pp. 52–53.

[24]Ibid., pp. 39–40.

[25]Ibid., p. 65.

[26]M. Scott Peck, *The Different Drum* (New York: Simon and Schuster, 1987), p. 188.

[27]J. Moltmann, source untraced